Beyond Churchianity

Beyond Churchianity

Insights from Japan for a World-Changing Christianity

FLOYD HOWLETT

With Foreword by the Very Rev. Bill Phipps

Hybrid Publishing Co-op Ltd.
Winnipeg, Canada

BEYOND CHURCHIANITY
Copyright © 2003 Floyd Howlett

All rights reserved. Except for brief quotations in a review, the reproduction, transmisson, or storage in a retreival system of any part of this publication without the prior written consent of the publisher is prohibited.

HYBRID PUBLISHING PRODUCERS CO-OPERATIVE LTD.
860 Mountain Avenue
Winnipeg, Canada   R2X 1C3
www.hybrid-publishing.ca

Hybrid books are available at special quanitity discounts for bulk purchases for sales promotions, fundraising, and educational needs. Book excerpts can also be created for special needs.

National Library of Canada Cataloguing in Publication Data

Howlett, Floyd, 1921-2003
   Beyond Churchianity : insights from Japan for a world-changing Christianity / Floyd Howlett ; with foreword by Bill Phipps.

Includes index.
ISBN 0-9689709-8-2

1. Howlett, Floyd, 1921-2003 2. Missionaries--Japan--Biography.
3. Missionaries--Canada--Biography. 4. United Church of Christ--Missions--Japan. 5. Northern Hokkaido Christian Centre--Biography. I. Title.

BV3457.H68A3 2003   266.5'834'092   C2003-911093-1

This book is typeset in 10.75/13 pt Palatino on pH neutral, 100% recycled paper.

Printed and bound in Canada by Hignell Printing.

CONTENTS

Foreword	vii
Introduction	1
1. Steps on a Long Faith Journey	5
2. Post-War Tokyo	19
3. Hokkaido Adventure	27
4. Hokkaido Challenges	57
5. Community Engagement	70
6. New Ways of Being Church	93
7. Engagement with Social & Political Issues	108
8. Doreen's Unique Talents	121
9. Family Reflections	145
10. Faith Insights	156
11. Dialogue with People of Other Faiths	184
12. Ongoing Challenges to Faith	203
Afterword	220
Index	221

FOREWORD

Floyd Howlett has written a memoir which builds upon his Japanese missionary experience while challenging the church to change in the 21st Century. Growing into liberation theology from both practical experience and academic debate, Floyd encourages us to broaden our scope while affirming the prophetic tradition.

I am delighted that he includes a chapter on faith traditions other than Christianity. I believe that our globalized world needs a multi-faith prophetic voice. It is no longer sufficient for ecumenical Christian voices to be heard on global issues such as peace, ecology, economic justice, HIV / AIDS, and trade. Both the World Council of Churches an its local counterparts do excellent work.

In Canada, ecumenical social justice done by KAIROS is essential, and provides a model of how churches with varying theologies can work together in public education and justice.

Yet in multi-cultural countries such as Canada, inter-faith action is the growing edge of social ethics from a spiritual perspective. Global organizations such as the World Conference on Religions for Peace and their local chapters are seeking to unite various faith traditions in strong public witness. I have been involved in an inter-faith effort called "Faith and the Common Good." It is based on the premise that the world's faith traditions share a common social ethic. They understand peace, justice, harmony, respect, wholeness, and other qualities of life as ethical imperatives of their greatly diverse theologies.

It is more difficult for governments and other public bodies to ignore multi-faith efforts for justive than the pleas of only one faith community. Organizing inter-faith action is a delicate and intense labour of love and sensitivity. The experience of many faiths (perhaps especially Aboriginal, Judaism and Islam) with Christianity has been negative, if not extremely oppressive. Christians need to be aware of the damage we have inflicted. It will take time to establish our credibility as a truly accepting and equal partner in the struggle for genuine peace and justice.

Meanwhile, the further development of a liberating theology within Christianity is a necessary and worthwhile project. A theology which holds personal spiritual health, together with courageous public witness, is what we need. In the face of growing "fundamentalism," this task becomes more urgent if we are to make any impact in the world. We need a theology of the love of God revealed in Christ which accepts and affirms the pathway to, and experience of, the divine found in other traditions.

We need stories of personal transformation leading to a reframing of both theology and action. Floyd tells his story with passion and integrity. He challenges us to remember and tell our own stories with a view to formulating a believable, responsive and transformative faith. Such a faith not only comforts and empowers the individual person, it pushes us to redemtive action for the sake of the world.

As much as I enjoyed reading Floyd's story, I was drawn into reflecting on my own life and how I understand my faith in engaging God's dream for the Earth.

The Very Rev. Bill Phipps
Former Moderator
United Church of Canada

INTRODUCTION

I am fully aware that the word "churchianity" does not occur in the dictionary but for me it sums up succinctly what has been the challenge of my life of separating authentic Christianity from a church centred pseudo-Christianity, far removed from the life and teaching of Jesus. The basis for the title, *Beyond Churchianity*, I take from words of the Dutch theologian J.C. Hoekendijk who challenged Church-centric missionary thinking about Christianity, saying it had gone astray because it revolves around an illegitimate centre. The proper alternative, he said, is to place the world and the Kingdom at the centre of our theology of mission. This same sense of dichotomy in the church has been my own experience working both within the church in Japan and in Canada.

From the time of the Roman Emperor Constantine, when the church became aligned with the state, it is my conviction that the church has been "off base," far removed from the central themes of justice, peace and love, so pivotal to all of Jesus' teaching and example. Attempts were made in the Reformation period to get back to the core, but for the most part they did not prove successful, ending up again with top-down, authoritarian churches of one kind or another. Although in this book I examine most closely churches in Japan, I believe, with few exceptions, that churches in Canada, the United States, Europe and around the world are caught in the same trap of being centred on their own well-being rather than on the needs of the world and of the communities of which they are a part.

Since they were often mirror images of western churches, Japanese churches have not been much different from their western counterparts. However, when my wife Doreen and I went to Japan in 1951 and were posted in the city of Nayoro on the northernmost island of Hokkaido we saw an opportunity to work towards building new types of church community that might avoid some of the pitfalls of churches in the past. Not only were we living on the northernmost island but we were also in a frontier region of northern Hokkaido. In this area, although there were a few isolated communities of Christians, there were very few churches. Here was an opportunity for being innovative and to build churches not so tied to the traditions of the past. Working with young Japanese ministers and lay people in Hokkaido, we experimented with trying to build alternate communities of faith looking outward to the communities rather than inward to the existence of the churches themselves.

This book tells the stories of our life in Japan and of working with our co-workers. We share our struggles, successes and failures as we sought to work cooperatively in this particular region. In many ways, the challenge of trying to move from "churchianity to Christianity" has also been the struggle of each of my mentors, both in Canada and Japan. The search for finding new ways of being the church in the world was one of the motivations that led Doreen and me to volunteer to go to Japan to offer ourselves as reconcilers with a people who had been thought of as enemies. In embarking on our "mission" to Japan we were conscious of the approach of many "missionaries" who had gone overseas with the idea of "evangelizing" the non-Christians and of building churches in the image of their home church or denomination. Fortunately for us, the United Church of Canada, which supported us, did not have this expectation. It sent us to Japan with the express purpose of building bridges of peace and supporting the existing Japanese church in its new mission in the post-war period.

The ideal was working in group or team ministries, of which both of us had some experience in Canada. We had always taken the position that "lone wolf" activity, however profound its purpose, can never be effective. For that reason we saw our roles as being listeners and learners rather than simply initiators. I welcomed the opportunity of having for Japanese co-workers, men and women who had a vision of collaboration and decision making by consensus. One example of this collaboration was the formation in the northern Hokkaido region, into three regional groupings of churches of the Kyodan (The United Church of Christ in Japan). The development of this innovative plan for being a different kind of church was carried out by a team of Japanese ministers and lay people in which we were equal participants.

The first chapter deals with some of the influences and the people who motivated Doreen and me to volunteer for service in Japan in 1951 under the auspices of the United Church of Canada. The focus is on the "why" of going to Japan. The second chapter is about making adjustments and meeting new friends in post-war Tokyo, where we spent two years in Japanese language study and where our first child, Dennis, was born.

The next several chapters might be called the Hokkaido saga. Hokkaido is the large northernmost island of Japan that was the venue of the major part of our work. It describes personal activities in our home, in the church and in the larger community. It also relates stories of the lives of Japanese co-workers and friends working together for a different kind of church.

The period of 1951 to 1981 was a time of major social change and political upheaval in Japan. We were fortunate to be there for most of that period except for the four one-year home assignments we spent in Canada. Chapter Seven relates our own engagement with some of the social and political issues of that period.

Chapter Eight is devoted to a tribute to my deceased wife Doreen, for the unique contributions she made in her life and work, both in Japan and Canada. In Chapter Nine our children tell their stories of growing up in Japan and the influences this had in choosing their careers.

In the remaining chapters I describe how life and work in Japan and studies in Canada changed my theological interpretation and my faith perspective. I especially examine liberation theologies from around the world and the place of interfaith dialogue in my own faith journey. I also describe the profound effect on the direction of my ministry by my participation in the Canadian Urban Training program that opened for me a whole new way of relating sociology to the Biblical perspective and to contemporary social issues.

I close *Beyond Churchianity* with a chapter seeking to draw out the implications of my faith journey as it relates to my present faith stance and examine some of the new directions I am still exploring.

Howlett family: Hilda, Floyd, Maurice, Ralph, and Wesley

1

STEPS ON A LONG FAITH JOURNEY

My faith journey began at my mother's knees. I say mother's because I see her faith having a stronger influence than that of my father. Mother Hilda had a venturesome spirit. She very much wanted to become a nurse. When she found that she didn't have the academic qualifications to take nurse's training in Canada she chose to enroll in a nurses' training school in Philadelphia, far away from home. She had a dream of becoming a missionary nurse in Africa but instead married Wesley, a farmer with whom she had grown up in the two room school house in West Montrose. Her dream became part of my later dream to serve in some capacity overseas.

My father, Wesley, was a pioneer. He was the first person in the West Montrose community to go to the Ontario Agricultural College in Guelph. He used his training to advance agricultural practice in our community. He took good care of the land he had received from his father. He had a love for the soil. He used little or no commercial fertilizer and instead renewed the soil with barnyard manure and careful crop rotation. He used scarcely any pesticides. From my father I gained a love for the soil and my interest in improving agriculture and the rural way of life.

Whereas mother was warm and outgoing, my father found it hard to express affection. I can't recall him ever praising myself or my two brothers, except when we occasionally overheard him speaking of our accomplishments to guests. Both my mother and father were active in lay leadership in the West Montrose United Church, especially in the Sunday School. Dad was, for a time, Superintendent of the Sunday School and later became the teacher of the adult Bible Class, a task which he took over from my mother's father, Clem Bowman. Whereas mother's faith was more accepting of people, dad tended to be more judgmental. He was very critical of the minister that followed the well respected Edis Fairbairn, over some disagreement, of which I have no idea now. Out of loyalty to the church, he continued to attend worship, but rather than shake hands with the minister after services he would slip out of the church by a back door.

Both mother and dad loved having young people in our home. After I became involved in the Presbytery and Conference Young People's Union I invited the leaders to our large farm home for week end conferences. Conferences like these were later expanded to become week-long residential "Winter Schools". Winter Schools had been a tradition in Hamilton Conference, held in various churches from year to year with the participants billeted in homes. The schools consisted of studies about the Bible, faith and daily living with time for fun and games. I took part in several Winter Schools after I graduated from High School. Since the usual number of participants was from 12 to 15, mother and dad invited the schools to be held in our large farm home. These early residential schools in the Howlett residence and other homes became precursors of Five Oaks, the Prairie Christian Training Centre and other residential leadership training schools that later grew up across the country. When mother and dad retired from the farm and moved to Elora they purposely bought a large house, so that they could accommodate the winter schools and other similar gatherings.

Mother's faith continued to be a strong influence on my faith journey right up until her death. She enfolded everyone she met in a mantle of love. The two years she spent with us in Nayoro, after my father died, was a great source of strength to both Doreen and me. It also provided an opportunity for our young sons, Dennis and Peter, to get to know the love of a grandmother.

When mother returned to Canada she joined my brother Ralph in the Hidden Springs Centre for people recovering from mental illness and alcoholism. She became "house mother" for the men's residence. There she shared her love with another group of people needing her care, recovering alcoholics. Ironically, all her life mother had a strong aversion to alcohol and its effects on society. She had been a member of the Women's

Christian Temperance Union (WCTU). However, when she came into contact with people with an alcoholic addiction, she had no trouble extending to them her accepting love - even if they fell off the wagon from time to time. Mother's love and acceptance of all sorts and conditions of life taught me much about being accepting of everyone.

Mother's love for people extended even beyond her death. In her will she expressed the wish that if it would be of any use she wanted to offer her body for medical science. To her, the spirit was far more important than the body. In accordance with her wishes, her body was given to a medical college with no request that it be interred in the cemetery beside her husband Wesley. Some years after her death when I was back in Canada, we three brothers, Maurice, Ralph and I, installed a plaque on my father's gravestone in the West Montrose Church Cemetery which reads:

> *In life she gave her heart*
> *That others might know love*
> *In death she gave her body*
> *That others might know healing*

Her faith continues to live on in my faith and the many lives she touched during her long life-time.

REV. EDIS FAIRBAIRN

I grew up in a rather typical conservative church community until the arrival of an unusual minister. The Rev. Edis Fairbairn was born in England, but had ministered in Bermuda during the First World War. Theologically he gave ultimate priority to the teachings of Jesus over the creeds and doctrines of the church and tried to shake people out of their literalistic reading of the Bible. Fairbairn's disillusionment with the aftermath of the First World War had made him a confirmed pacifist. In his book, *Apostate Christendom*, he tells the story of soldiers ordered to engage in bayonet drill who came to him when he was Acting Chaplain in Bermuda:

"Tell us please," they said, "how we can continue to be Christian and still do the things we are ordered to do?"

When war broke out again in 1939 he was unalterably opposed to war and to the churches' support of the war effort. He, along with Rev. James Finlay and about 150 other persons, ministers and lay, drafted and signed a "Witness Against War" declaration. Their declaration was based on a series of pronouncements made by the United Church General Councils in the pre-war period, affirming "the unchanging conviction that war is contrary to the mind of Christ." Fairbairn castigated the United Church for not living up to its earlier pronouncements. As a result of his courageous stance he was voted out of a large, affluent church and was forced to spend the rest of his ministry on a small rural charge.

During the war years and after, I kept in touch with Fairbairn and eagerly read his books and newsletters that had a considerable influence on my own thinking and actions with regard to a Christian's responsibility in the face of a nation's participation in war. Fairbairn's three-fold emphases on living out the teachings of Jesus, his rejection of war and his call for taking responsibility for building the Kingdom of God through a new social order left an unforgettable impression on my faith and action. This was the unforgettable lesson I learned from Fairbairn - working for world peace also involved the obligation of working for a new economic and political order and the reconstruction of a just and peaceful society.

Even though he was not properly recognized during his lifetime I look upon Edis Fairbairn as a giant of the faith, a man ahead of his time, a prophet without the honour he deserved. Edis Fairbairn started me on a faith odyssey that has had continuing repercussions throughout my life's journey.

UNITED CHURCH YOUNG PEOPLES' UNION
During my teen years there was a small but very active United Church Young People's Union in the West Montrose Church that met in the church every Friday evening. At that time the

Y.P.U. was the largest youth organization in Canada with 2,600 local unions and about 56,000 members. I was privileged to be able to participate in the organization at the local, Presbytery and Conference levels. These activities helped to widen my vision of the Christian faith and the world scene and were a valuable training ground for personality development and leadership skills. The meetings of the Y.P.U. were conducted democratically with the aim of involving all members in leadership roles. Members prepared study and worship programmes. The programmes included the essentials of the Christian faith, politics and social issues, institutions and customs of countries in which the United Church was involved in "mission." They also provided the basis for a liberal education which was an invaluable preparation for my entry into college.

During this period I also attended three Y.P.U. Executive Leadership Camps at Ryerson Beach on Lake Erie. In addition to the fun and fellowship I enjoyed and the many new close friendships I made at these camps, I was inspired by the challenges of a number of "theme speakers." The ones I remember most vividly are the Rev. Bev Oaten who later founded the "Five Oaks" church leadership centre at Paris, Ontario and Dr. Gordon Agnew, who had served as a missionary dentist in West China. Gordon and other "returned missionaries" helped to turn my thoughts to the possibility of overseas missionary service.

DR. ARNOT ORTON

Dr. Arnot Orton, my Old Testament Professor during the first two years at Emmanuel College made a significant contribution to my Biblical understanding on my faith journey. In addition to leading us through the labyrinth of Old Testament literature, he was like an Old Testament prophet himself as he vehemently expounded the social teachings of Amos, Isaiah, Jeremiah. He insisted that prophecy did not end with the Old Testament. He challenged us to be prophets denouncing the injustices and evils of our own day. He inspired me, not merely to speak out prophetically but also to work for a world based on justice and compassion and love. Not only was Dr. Orton a respected teacher, but he also became a personal friend.

SUMMER MISSION FIELDS

My own "mission" for the two summers of 1942 and 1943 was as a student minister in Saskatchewan. The first summer I spent at Iffley, Saskatchewan, north of North Battleford. Sunday church services were in four schoolhouses, two services each Sunday with children's meetings in the schools after school during the week. Transportation was by horseback on the "mission horse," Slick. Slick knew his way around better than I. One night as I was taking a short-cut home over a dim prairie trail through a farmer's field darkness descended and I didn't know the way home. Slick stayed on the trail and stopped when he came to a barbed wire gate to let me dismount, open and close the gate, mount and continue on my way.

One interesting part of my work was to visit every family in the region. One of these visits had an international dimension. One day I called on the Von Kameke family. They had come from Germany seven years previously. Since this was in the midst of the war some people in the community thought they might be spies. Nothing could be further from the truth. They had come to Canada to get away from Hitler's Naziism. They had two little girls, Eva and Hannah. The first day I visited I found Mrs. Von Kameke all alone with the two girls trying to look after the farm herself. Her husband was in the hospital having an eye operation. She was worried about getting the harvest in. Since during the war help for farmers was scarce the Mission Board had given permission for summer students to assist with the harvest for up to twelve days. Several days later, when I visited Mr. Von Kameke in the hospital he was overjoyed to know that I would be able to help him. By the time the harvest began he was out of the hospital and able to cut the grain himself. I spent a total of nearly two weeks stooking the sheaves. While there we had some interesting conversations about Germany and the war. Both Mr. and Mrs. Von Kameke spoke excellent English. Mr. Von Kameke remarked, "Here in Canada we have freedom, but it is hard to imagine what it is like to live in a country where everything you read, hear and speak is brought about by propaganda." Living and working with the Von Kamekes was the highlight of that summer, since the conversations with them gave me a new understanding of those who live under totalitarian regimes.

The experience of serving on two summer mission fields helped me to think through and articulate my faith more clearly when relating to a wide variety of people. This was a further preparation for my eventual mission overseas.

REV. JAMES M. FINLAY
The early influence of Edis Fairbairn on my life and faith was deepened and enhanced by a seven-year association with the Rev. Jim Finlay during my years in Toronto at Victoria College and Emmanuel College. Finlay's ministry can be summed up in the phrase, "speaking the mind of Christ to the issues of the time." To him, as to Rev. Edis Fairbairn, one of the great issues of the time was the outbreak of World War II. To Finlay, war was "against the mind of Christ" and needed to be resisted with all our powers. He and his close friend, Edis Fairbairn were the two people most responsible for the drafting and distribution of the Peace Manifesto signed by 75 ministers and a similar number of lay people.

Like Edis Fairbairn, Finlay also faced a crisis when a group within Carlton St. United Church tried to dismiss him from its leadership. Unlike Fairbairn, however, he was able to ride out the storm. When it came to the test he was given an overwhelming vote of confidence, even though many did not fully agree with him. In the two years he had been with them they had come to realize the strength of his convictions and the sincere warmth of his ministry.

It was undoubtedly the strong anti-war stance of these two outstanding men that led me to request postponement of military service so that I could continue my studies in College. The only way in which I could do this, however, was to participate in the Canadian Officers Training Corps on campus. I agonized over this for some time. Some of my classmates had signed up and gone overseas. Others chose to declare themselves "conscientious objectors" and had accepted "alternative service" in work camps in northern Ontario and British Columbia. Several had been allowed to join the Friends' Ambulance Service with Dr. Bob McLure, the famous China missionary doctor, going to West China by way of the Burma Road to bring medical aid to the Chinese people who were being bombed by the Japanese military.

In September of 1943 I wrote in my diary: "As far as I can see, war is contrary to the mind of Christ. Believing that, what should I do? Should I give up my scholarship, jeopardize my college education, cut myself off from the activity in the College based Young People's Forward Movement working with youth groups throughout Ontario, just because of a requirement of several hours a week military training? Or should I acquiesce in the training, as long as it means no active participation in war? What would Jesus do?" I may have compromised by participating in the military drills, but at the same time I committed myself to what I called "a lifetime of alternative service to war participation."

Finlay's faith was based on a practical and situational theology that was aimed primarily at trying to discover through prayer, dialogue with other concerned Christians, and the Spirit of Jesus what were the primary issues of the times and the actions required to bring about a more just and peaceful world.

Another of the "issues of the times" with which he felt compelled to "seek the mind of Christ" came after Pearl Harbour and the outbreak of the war with Japan. He castigated the government for the way Japanese Canadians in British Columbia had been arrested, their property seized, and families separated before being sent to internment camps in the interior of British Columbia. He continually worked for their release and called upon churches throughout Canada to sponsor Japanese families and welcome them into their fellowship. Unfortunately, at first there were few churches, apart from Carlton St. Church, that responded to this appeal.

I was present in the Carlton St. United Church congregation when Jim Finlay was preaching those challenging sermons and they had a profound effect on my life. It was not long before I arranged for the Ogawa family, a grandmother, father, mother and two children, to go to my farm home in West Montrose, where my mother and father welcomed them and gave them employment on the farm. Not long after this I became the "student assistant" at Carlton with a major responsibility for leadership in the Young People's Union and the Saturday Night Dance and Recreation Club for young people. Because Carlton St. Church welcomed them so warmly, many of the Japanese Canadian young people came to Carlton and became my close friends. This association caused me to think seriously about the possibility, after the war, of becoming a reconciler for peace between the two warring nations.

This period from 1941 to 1948, working with Finlay and the Carlton St. congregation, helped to shape my faith and action for the days ahead. Not only did it confirm my commitment to peace and non-violent action but also instilled in my heart a passion against any kind of discrimination or exploitation, wherever it would raise its ugly head.

PROFESSOR NORTHROP FRYE

From 1941 to 1948 I attended the United Church Victoria and Emmanuel Colleges in Toronto. I enjoyed these years immensely. I found the courses at Victoria, especially English and Philosophy, fascinating and mind expanding. The one professor that stands out most dramatically was the eminent scholar Northrop Frye. At that time "Norrie Frye" was a young but very popular professor. I took a stimulating course on Spenser and Milton. At the outset of this course he stated: "Spenser's *Fairie Queen* and Milton's *Paradise Lost* are two of the greatest achievements in English Literature outside Shakespeare." This course opened my mind to epic poetry and the whole range of philosophical and religious thought represented by these two great poets and to Frye's incisive interpretations.

Frye's greatest impact, however, came through participation in a Student Christian Movement study group on poetry, myth and metaphor in the Bible that took place in his office. A group of eight met weekly in sessions where, using cross-reference Bibles, he helped us trace recurring myths and metaphors through the Bible from Genesis to Revelation. He helped us see that the Bible is written in the language of literature and that its stories and writings were not meant to be taken literally but poetically and metaphorically. We began to understand that the mythical stories of creation, birth and resurrection had deeper meanings when read as poetry rather than taken as fact or doctrine. This had a profound effect on my later attempts to teach the Bible to Japanese people who were encountering the Bible for the first time.

I give thanks to Northrop Frye for helping to release my imagination and enabling me to read the Bible as a living document speaking to any culture in any generation. I credit Edis Fairbairn and Norie Frye for helping me to go to Japan with an open mind. It saved me from falling into the pitfall of many preachers and missionaries who believe they have to declare Christianity as the "only way" or even the "best way" to God and spirituality. They prepared me to accept happily the Japanese Buddhist saying that in matters of faith, "there are many ways to the top of Mount Fuji."

The tutelage of Fairbairn and Frye prepared me for entry into other faith perspectives and at the same time gave me a deeper understanding of my faith heritage. These were among the greatest gifts I took with me to Japan.

REV. GEORGE AFFLECK

The friend and mentor who no doubt had the greatest influence in overcoming my doubts about attempting to work within a church structure and in considering overseas ministry was George Affleck. I got to know George shortly after he had graduated from Emmanuel College when he was one of the leaders in a new faith and outreach initiative started by about twenty students from Emmanuel and Victoria Colleges in February of 1939. The students were distressed by what they saw happening in the world and in the church. In the face of tremendous world challenges the church was failing to live up to its mission of being a light to the world in the midst of darkness. In the church there was a serious drop in candidates for the ministry, a big drop in membership in Sunday Schools, a decrease in church attendance and a fifty per cent decline in missionary contributions. They believed it could only be turned around by the power of a living God working through a "Forward Movement" beginning with young people. They called their group "The Young People's Forward Movement."

I may not now entirely agree with its early theology or its world view of mission, however, the Young People's Forward Movement did have a considerable influence on my own life and on the lives of the many young people it touched. It changed their directions and inspired them to take leadership roles in many areas of the life of the world. In my faith journey it helped me to critique older forms of mission and to seek new ways of being the church in the world.

This group of students met regularly for study and prayer and developed a plan for sending out teams of students to the young people's groups of the United Church and to summer church youth camps to share their vision. Their strategy was to form "fellowship groups" of committed and trained Christians to act as revitalizing centres in church and community. George Affleck and his fellow graduate Bert Scott were among the first of these teams. They agreed to devote two years after graduation to the work of the Forward Movement, visiting churches and camps. I met George and Bert first when attending the Ryerson Beach Young People's Leadership Camp on Lake Erie. They were inspiring and challenging leaders. They urged campers to go back to their own communities and to start fellowship groups for their own growth in faith, and for more effective outreach and service to their own churches and communities.

Several participants of that camp, including me, took up the challenge and drew together interested young people from Kitchener/Waterloo churches and from my home church of West Montrose. We met weekly in Trinity United Church, Kitchener for our own fellowship group in which we studied together the book *Discipleship* by the British author Dr. Leslie Weatherhead, relating faith to issues of daily life. For many of us, several years in this group brought about changes in direction in our lives as we decided on new careers or found new ways of serving more faithfully in our own communities.

During this period George Affleck came to my home church in West Montrose several times. We had long talks as I was agonizing about my future. I was disillusioned by what I saw in the church. I agreed with Fairbairn that the church by its failure to stand up against the evil of war and by accepting the standards of the world was abandoning its principles and becoming apostate. To me, much of the church as I knew it had given up on the basic tenets of justice, peace and true compassion. How could I work within a structure which was so hypocritical? But as I looked around at alternates I wondered, "Where could I find a structure that is any better?"

It was at this point that George gave me a new vision of how working in small groups or cells, as we had been doing, we could bypass the retrogressive structures of the church and act as leavening groups in both church and society. He encouraged me to attend Victoria College as a candidate for the ministry in the United Church of Canada.

This I chose to do after having spent three years at home working with my father and mother on the farm. My father gave me several piglets which I raised and sold to pay for my tuition fees to college. In the fall of 1941 I entered Victoria College and lived in a Campus Cooperative Residence. We shared the costs and the work of running the residence, including helping with meals. The experience of working in a co-op, where we also studied the basic principles of the British "Rochdale" system of cooperatives, was in itself an invaluable preparation for my later work with farm young people in Hokkaido.

MINISTRY IN THE ESTERHAZY PASTORAL CHARGE

After graduation from Emmanuel College in the spring of 1948 I was ordained and appointed to serve as minister to three churches in Saskatchewan, Esterhazy, Tantallon and Hazelcliffe, in what was known as the Esterhazy Pastoral Charge.

The roles of clergy and laity within the church was one which concerned me from my college days. I did not feel comfortable with the role that most clergy had taken on within the church. The issue had come to the fore when we were to get our graduation pictures taken. Should I or should I not wear a "Roman Collar" for the photograph? All the other graduates planned on wearing one. I discussed the matter with one of the professors and he convinced me that there might be occasions where it was appropriate, so I finally consented. When I got to Esterhazy I compromised. I would wear the collar for weddings and funerals, but at no other times. Gradually I came to feel that even that much made a barrier between myself and the parishioners. How could the laity really feel that they had a ministry just as important as the "minister" as long as this distinction existed? After leaving Esterhazy and going to Japan I never wore the collar again. It stayed in the bottom of the trunk for many years until I finally burnt it with the garbage. Since that time I have never worn gown or collar.

    I was expected to be in Esterhazy before the first Sunday of July, 1948 to begin my ministry. I bought a second-hand car in Toronto and drove to the West. When I arrived in Esterhazy I went to the post office where I met Vernon Flook, the Post Master and also an elder in the United Church. When I asked how to get to my new home in the United Church manse, I got my first big surprise. A young boy of about nine had just walked into the post office. Vernon Flook said, "Here's Danny Beveridge, the son of the former minister, whose family is still living in the manse. He will show you the way." When we got to the manse I met Danny's father, Tom, his mother, Mae and baby brother John. This situation, which could have been quite uncomfortable, actually turned out quite amicably. I boarded with them, lived in the house, and looked after the lovely big garden they had planted. Tom gave me lots of information about the churches and the people in the parish. Tom, who had been left without a church for health reasons, regained his health and by September was able to move to a small church near Regina. Our friendship continued over the years and every time we returned to Canada we arranged to spend some time with Tom, Mae and the children.

    I learned that a rural pastor in Saskatchewan had to travel great distances and get to know a wide variety of people of many nationalities, often living in isolated communities. Every Sunday I had services in three churches, morning, afternoon and evening. After a rain some of the country roads turned to "gumbo" mud and became almost impassable.

Although we enjoyed our ministry in Saskatchewan immensely, and developed many close friendships, the United Church of Christ in Japan was calling for help from overseas churches and personnel to help them re-build after the war. We felt that the need for our services in Japan was greater than the need in Canada. In addition, going to Japan would provide us with an opportunity to fulfill our heartfelt desire to work for reconciliation with the people of Japan who had been considered our enemies. This would be a practical way in which to work for peace in the world and fulfill my commitment to a lifetime of alternative service.

In going to Japan we asked the congregations of the Esterhazy Pastoral Charge to consider us as their representatives to the churches and the people of Japan. We promised to keep in touch and to visit them again each time we returned to Canada for home assignment. Throughout all our years in Japan our hearts were full of thankfulness for the love and support from the congregations back home on the Esterhazy Pastoral Charge.

After a summer visiting families and packing dozens of boxes, the Overseas Mission Board sent us across Canada by train and down the west coast of the United States to San Francisco. There, in early September of 1951, we boarded a Norwegian freighter and began our perilous journey across the Pacific Ocean.

2

POST-WAR TOKYO

In September 1951 we were on a Norwegian freighter en route to Japan when we ran into a typhoon. We were confined to our cabin for two days. The smorgasbord food in the diner soon lost its appeal. Our fellow-missionary companions, Evelyn and Lloyd Graham, were too sea-sick to get out of bed. Although we weren't much better off, Doreen and I looked after their six month old Adrienne. As the ship rolled and tossed we asked ourselves many times "Were we fools to accept this challenge to work with the United Church of Christ in Japan?" After being married in November of 1948, Doreen and I had three happy years ministering in Saskatchewan. We made many good friends and hated to leave them behind. We enjoyed our work in the churches and in the communities where Doreen led a "Canadian Girls in Training" group and where I helped to manage a boys' hockey team. Now we asked ourselves, "Why did we leave a secure position among people we love to offer ourselves for lifetime service in post-war Japan?"

We began to further question our sanity as we learned more about what we would face. Lloyd had already spent some time in Japan as a translator with the U.S. occupation forces immediately after the war. He had seen the bombed out cities and the vast numbers of hungry and homeless people. He had travelled to the northern outpost of Hokkaido where he had met people who had never before seen a white person. Would we really be accepted by a people who had looked upon all North Americans as enemies?

After the storm Lloyd taught us our first Japanese words, "Ohayo" for good morning and "Sayonara" for goodbye. Were we crazy to think we could learn a difficult language like Japanese at age thirty? Would we ever be able to understand Japanese and communicate with the Japanese people?

At the end of two weeks at sea we arrived in Yokohama harbour to be met on board by Ernest Bott, a pre-war United Church missionary who had been one of the first to return to Japan after the war. He took us ashore on a motor launch where we met his wife Edith. On the drive to their Tokyo home we saw crowds of people in front of their tiny paper-shuttered homes. We noticed the many tiny shops on the narrow streets. The Botts took us to their spacious western style home that had been built for them by the United Church of Canada in a bombed-out area of the city. We spent two weeks with the Botts, during which time they recounted many stories of both pre-war and post-war Japan and oriented us to our new life.

The Botts helped us move into the pre-fabricated house which had been shipped from Vancouver for Alfred and Jean Stone and their two boys shortly after the war. The Stones were also pre-war missionaries with long experience who were now back in Canada. We were to live in this house for our two years of language study in Tokyo. The house was in the midst of a Japanese community where no one spoke English. As we struggled with the Japanese language and with what we later learned was "culture shock" we experienced emotions ranging from fear and discouragement to exhilaration and anticipation.

GETTING SETTLED

Our two year stay in Tokyo, September 1951 to August 1953, for language study and orientation to life in Japan, was an interlude between our pastoral work in Esterhazy and our new mission task in Hokkaido. It was a most valuable preparation for a challenging task for which we were ill-prepared. Later missionary arrivals were given a month of orientation and preparation in Canada for living in a new culture. We had to discover our own way. It was not until our first home assignment five years later that we had the term "culture shock" explained to us. Then we exclaimed, "Oh, was that what we were going through? We thought that those difficult experiences happened only to us."

One of the customs that frustrated us was always taking off shoes when going into a house. Even at the church we had to take off our shoes and put on slippers provided for us in the entrance way. Invariably they were much too small. Another new custom was to always scrub the whole body before getting in to the deep, steaming hot Japanese bath-tub. Of course we had to quickly learn how to eat with chopsticks, since in most homes and restaurants cutlery was not provided. We also had to get used to gift giving customs. We found that when we gave gifts to friends, before long we invariably got a much fancier gift back. Sometime if we admired some item in a home, they would insist on presenting it to us, even if it was a long-treasured family heirloom. Another frustration was that in learning the Japanese language we discovered that verbs come at the end of sentences, rather than in the middle as in English.

At first, we were fascinated by the new sights and sounds and smells of Tokyo. We did walking tours of shrines and temples and explored the little shopping districts. We took pictures of the "kamishibai man" gathering children around him on the street to tell stories using large picture cards and then selling sweets. We got used to being wakened early in the morning to the call of the "natto" pedlar selling his fermented soy beans, a favourite breakfast delight. We got to appreciate Japanese food from the delicious "sukiyaki," beef and vegetables cooked on an iron dish over a charcoal brazier, to the more unpalatable dried squid. As we wandered around Tokyo we found whole blocks that had still not been re-built, even though this was six years after the end of the war. I remember seeing the ruins of a church with nothing left but the entrance. Crowded along the river banks were shacks of the homeless.

On the streets we saw the Jeeps of the U.S. and Australian forces, since this was still "Occupied Japan." General Douglas MacArthur was in charge. There was little unrest, since most people were happy with the new "peace constitution" developed by the Japanese government with the guidance of the US. This constitution promised that Japan would never again build up armed forces capable of launching a war. Most Japanese had seen too much of war already.

Towards the end of our first year the occupation was lifted and full powers were turned over to the Japanese government.

On the day of the decree there were some demonstrations celebrating the "liberation" and a few army Jeeps were overturned and burned, but for the most part the transition was peaceful. In a letter to friends in Canada in July of 1952 I made these remarks: "I still feel that the greatest internal danger to Japan lies in the conservative nationalistic elements which are trying to regain power and which use the threat of communism to stamp out some of the liberties which have been gained so far." Communism was never a real threat. We ourselves soon found that many of the communists were among the most ardent peace activists.

LEARNING THE LANGUAGE

On arrival in Tokyo, toward the end of September, we immediately enrolled in the Naganuma Japanese Language School. During the first year this was housed in a Baptist Church about one half hour away by Jeep. Our class had been made up of a group of six "late-comers." Since the church had run out of space we had to put up with a drafty stair landing for our classroom. From the first day our language teacher spoke nothing but Japanese. We would get frustrated at times, but once a week the Principal, who spoke some English, would come to the class and try to answer our questions. We borrowed language records from the school to work on proper pronunciation. Listening to the same records over and over was boring, but was worth it in the end.

The first year of language school was completed the end of June, so we remained, during the summer months, the hottest and muggiest time of the year, in the Gazenbo Cho house in Tokyo. The house was in a narrow valley with few summer breezes. The days were hot and oppressive. We would get up early to try to study some Japanese before the worst of the heat hit us. Doreen was pregnant so the stifling heat affected her particularly hard. The baby was expected toward the end of August. We had arranged for the birth at the Tokyo Seventh Day Adventist hospital where there was a U.S. doctor on staff. On the morning of August 26th Doreen awoke about 3 a.m. with labour pains. We got in the Jeep and headed for the hospital through the almost deserted streets. We made it in time, but none too soon since baby Dennis was born about an hour later. He was healthy but a bit scrawny, since Doreen had not been able to eat well because of the heat. When Doreen got home, in about four days, Edith Bott came over to help with the bathing and looking after Dennis. The second Sunday after the birth we took Dennis to the Tokyo Union Church for a dedication service along with newborn babies of our close language school friends, the Brownlees, the Bascoms and the Skillmans. During the second year of language school we four families got together frequently to share our joys and struggles and to watch each other's children grow and develop. I have delightful memories of a barbecue in our lovely back yard, with the infants and parents. It was like an oasis of freedom and relaxation where the tensions of second-language acculturation were temporarily forgotten.

By the second year the language school had moved to a brand new building in the Shibuya area. I continued to commute, but Doreen stayed home with Dennis and studied with a tutor. However, with a baby to look after, studying at home was not easy for Doreen. She never felt that she had mastered the language enough before we had to move out on our own. Thirty years of age is not an ideal time to start learning a new language. Although I learned to read and write, I never really became proficient in the written language. I put my main effort into trying to communicate through speech. Even after we moved to Hokkaido we continued language study with a tutor several times a week. Learning Japanese was our biggest hurdle in becoming accustomed to Japan.

Although we had no English speaking neighbours living close by, our daily living was greatly assisted by Yasuko-san, a Japanese helper who had also been "bequeathed" to us along with the mission house by the on-home-assignment Stones. Yasuko-san and her high school age brother and a cousin lived in a small attached room. Although her English was rather limited we managed to communicate so that she could do most of the buying of rationed rice and other local foods as well as helping with the meals and housework. This allowed us to devote more time to the study of Japanese.

ERNEST AND EDITH BOTT

Edith and Ernest Bott were our mentors and life-line during our first year in Tokyo. The Botts came to Japan in 1921 and stayed for some time after the war broke out. Under the Japanese military regime, spies followed them around on the streets and even attended church services to make notes on what they were preaching. Gradually they became an embarrassment to their Japanese church co-workers who were questioned on their movements and actions. When life became more and more precarious in the midst of the war they were finally evacuated in 1942.

Ernie was the first Canadian missionary to be sent back to Japan in 1945 after the war. His job was to co-ordinate emergency relief services. He was appointed director of an ecumenical relief agency known as LARA - Licensed Agency for Relief in Japan. The purpose of LARA was to provide food, clothing, medical and school supplies to devastated communities all over Japan. Ernie Bott threw himself into this task unstintingly, travelling in crowded trains all over Japan. It is estimated that fourteen million people benefited from the program. In *Requiem From The Sea*, a biography of Alfred Stone, Niihori Kuniji says "(Ernie Bott) had to be a superman, distributing relief all around the country while the transportation system was still in the process of being rebuilt. Bott's commitment to his work probably ended up shortening his life."

In his pre-war days in Tokyo, drawing on his social work training, Ernie Bott helped to found the Airindan (the house of love) social service Centre in Nippori, a poorer area of Tokyo. Shortly after we arrived in Tokyo Ernie persuaded me to teach an English conversation class in the Airindan one night a week. Although I did not have time to get involved in the other parts of the work of the Airindan, this experience helped me to see another aspect of the life and work of the church among the poor in inner city Tokyo. Since Ernie was busy travelling, delivering relief supplies and helping to get kindergarten and churches re-established in many areas of Japan, we did not often see him. His wife Edith was our mainstay during the early months. Edith had rejoined Ernie after the war in the fall of 1946. They built a lovely home and it was to this home that the new, younger missionaries like ourselves were welcomed as they began coming to Japan. Edith helped us settle into our new home in the district of Gazenbo-Cho and introduced us to the Intermission Services basic supply store and the Australian Forces canteen where we obtained western style foods not available in Japanese stores.

I was deeply distressed the morning of March 2nd, 1952, on phoning Edith, to hear, "Oh, Ernie just died." We rushed over and were the first "Westerners" to arrive to help and comfort Edith. Ernie had a slight heart attack some months earlier, and had slowed down a bit from his busy pace, but this second attack was fatal. We were present at the huge funeral, held in the Assembly Hall of the Toyo Eiwa Mission School, attended by a large crowd of mourners from all walks of life. There were glowing tributes from church and government leaders alike to the unstinting service he had given to the Japanese nation.

Edith continued in Tokyo helping with relief work for a number of years after Ernie's death. Edith was still our main support during our stay in Tokyo. After coming back to Canada we were happy to keep up our friendship with Edith. I visited her in Toronto shortly before her death in 1996 at the age of 101. Both Ernie and Edith Bott remained an inspiration to us as we began our mission task in Japan. Their dedication and obvious love for the Japanese people made them role models as we took up our own work. Their knowledge of Japanese history and long experience in the life of the Japanese church helped us to understand better the milieu in which we were to find our own life's work.

OUR SOCIAL LIFE IN TOKYO

Our social life while in Tokyo was rather limited. From time to time we visited Lloyd and Evelyn Graham, our travel companions across the Pacific, who were posted to a social service centre in Zushi, south of Yokohama. Lloyd had previous Japanese language training so was able to go right to work. For Evelyn it was not so easy. She had to begin studying Japanese with a tutor at home. Lloyd's training in social work was invaluable for the reorganization of the social service activities of the centre. Zushi was a port city with a large U.S. military base. Wealth, poverty and prostitution were all a part of the social spectrum to which the Zushi Centre was called to minister. The first Japanese church service we attended was in the Zushi Centre a few weeks after our arrival in Japan. The service was, of course, entirely in Japanese. There were some familiar hymn tunes, but we didn't understand the words. The sermon was incomprehensible. We asked ourselves, how will we ever understand, let alone lead worship and preach in Japanese?

From time to time we had pot-luck suppers with missionary friends from the language school. On Sundays we often attended the Tokyo Union Church English service together. We frequently gathered at each others homes for fun and fellowship. Four families all had babies during the second year, so that was another bond that held us together. We became close friends with one of these couples, Wally and Helen Brownlee since they, along with ourselves, were stationed in Hokkaido after language study. They were especially important to our family, since in many ways they became like surrogate parents to our children when they had to move away from home to attend English speaking schools at the Junior High School level in Sapporo and then for High School in Tokyo. While the Brownlees were in Sapporo, Dennis stayed with them for his second year of Junior High School at the Hokkaido International School. When they later moved to Tokyo their home was next door to the dormitory for missionary children, where our three, Dennis, Peter and Susan lived for several years while attending the American School in Japan. The Brownlee's children and ours were close friends and Helen and Wally were loving parents for all of them.

3

HOKKAIDO ADVENTURE

Christmas 1952 saw us flying north to the fulfilment of a long time dream. We were on our way to check out the prospects for a possible mission appointment to Nayoro, a small city in the northern part of Hokkaido. A request had come to the Cooperative Evangelism Committee from the Rev. Kiyoji Tamura of the United Church of Christ congregation in Nayoro for a missionary couple to work with himself and the Nayoro Church. He had a dream of expanding the outreach of the church in the whole northern region of Hokkaido where, although there were some Christian people, there were very few churches. The prospect looked enticing. This was an area to which no missionaries had been sent before. The possibility existed to undertake innovative work, not tied to the traditions of the past. Repatriated families from Manchuria and the Sakhalin Island were being settled in pioneer communities in the region and many of these needed social support, training and leadership skills. In other parts of Japan several rural training and conference centres had already been successfully established. A rural conference centre had been proposed for northern Hokkaido in Nayoro. This was the challenge and adventure we had been waiting for.

We also looked forward to visiting Ian and Virginia MacLeod and Don and Ruth Clugston who were just beginning their assignments in Hokkaido. Ian had been a classmate in Emmanuel College. The MacLeods had begun work in the city of Otaru, west of Sapporo, eighteen months previously. The Clugstons had just spent two months in Asahigawa.

We took off from the green grass of Tokyo and three hours later landed in a fairyland covered with two feet of snow. Doreen exclaimed, "This is the first time I have really felt at home in Japan." Ian met us in Sapporo and drove us to their home in Otaru, about an hour away. The MacLeods had moved to Otaru, just after we had arrived in Tokyo the year before, so were already in the midst of many church activities there.

During the days before Christmas we were given an insight into just how busy a missionary's life can become. We observed a continuous stream of Japanese visitors coming to the MacLeod home. Many of them bore gifts, which spoke well of the way in which the MacLeods had won their way into the hearts of the people of their community within one year. We got a thrill out of seeing them entertain about forty of the neighbourhood children at a Christmas party. Many of these children heard the story of the birth of Jesus for the first time. We also shared a young people's party on Christmas Eve. Christmas day was most enjoyable, especially when we were able to celebrate it with the MacLeods' three children and our own baby.

The day after Christmas we went to Asahigawa in central Hokkaido to visit the Clugstons. If we were to go to Nayoro they would be our closest English speaking neighbours, and their three children would be Dennis's closest Western playmates. The Clugstons were working with two churches of the United Church of Christ in Asahigawa. Don and Ruth had first been sent to China as missionaries, partly because Ruth's parents had been China missionaries, and she had grown up in China. However, with the Communist take-over they had been evacuated from China and sent to Kobe for Japanese language training and then appointed to work in Asahigawa. The Clugstons were getting used to living in an old drafty Japanese style house. It was good to get to know them and to be assured that we would have some Canadian friends not too far away if we decided to go to Nayoro.

While staying with the Clugstons I took a day trip by train to Nayoro, about two and one half hours further north. I was joined by Alfred Stone who had returned to Japan from home assignment in Canada and the Rev. Tsuneta, the minister of the "Roku Jo" (Sixth Avenue) church in Asahigawa. We were met at the Nayoro station by Rev. Kiyoji Tamura who showed us the church and took us around town to meet some of the church elders and the Mayor. The church was a western style church built about 40 years previously by a Christian lumber mill owner who had been among the early settlers of this town at the beginning of the century. We were attracted by the city, of about 25,000 people, situated in a valley with low mountains on either side. The wide streets, unlike most Japanese towns in Honshu, were laid out in blocks, but most of the streets were as yet unpaved. The church people seemed anxious to have us come and said they were already looking for a suitable house, or failing that a lot on which a house could be built. We were favourably impressed and said that we were looking forward to working with them. We would be the most northerly missionaries in Japan, serving a territory stretching about 300 kilometres to Wakkanai, the northernmost city in Japan.

THE UNITED CHURCH OF CHRIST IN JAPAN
It might be of interest to look briefly at the formation of the United Church of Christ in Japan, to which we had been sent as co-operating missionaries, and the way in which missionary assignments were decided. Appointments of missionaries were made through a rather complicated system of collaboration between the Nihon Kirisuto Kyodan (The United Church of Christ in Japan) and mission representatives of eight cooperating denominations from overseas - seven from the United States plus the United Church of Canada forming the "Interboard Committee for Christian Work in Japan." This Committee in turn worked with the Japanese church through a "Council of Cooperation."

The Nihon Kirisuto Kyodan had an interesting history. For many years before the war, discussions had taken place between some of the main churches about union. However these plans had never come to fruition. When the war broke out, the Japanese military, suspicious of the churches and not wanting to work with a plethora of denominations, decreed that churches must amalgamate. Catholic churches were allowed to remain as one group but all Protestant churches were forced into union. In total, about 30 different Protestant groups were formed into one church - the Nihon Kirisuto Kyodan. Some of the churches which had been working for union welcomed the amalgamation. Other churches deplored being forced into a union they did not want. At the end of the war, with government restrictions lifted, the opportunity was given to withdraw. A few of these, the Episcopal Church, the Baptists, the Presbyterian churches of Hokkaido and some evangelical groups broke their ties to the United Church of Christ in Japan and went back to being independent denominations. However, many of the churches with a long history of working together in Japan did remain in the union. Among these were the Methodists, most of the Presbyterians, the Congregationalists, the Disciples of Christ, and some Pentecostal churches.

Our work was also carried out in close cooperation with missionaries of the seven United States churches that were a part of the Interboard Committee for Christian Work in Japan. The assignment of missionaries was carried out through the joint body of the Council of Cooperation. First, each district of the Japanese church sent in lists of locations in which they desired missionaries to be placed. At that time from among fifteen districts there was a total of 74 requests but only 16 missionaries were available for what was called pastoral work, that is, direct work with Japanese churches. Others were appointed to education or social work positions.

Our preference for Hokkaido was taken into consideration because Hokkaido was in many ways like Canada in climate and history. In some respects northern Hokkaido resembled the Canadian west, since it had only been opened up for settlement in the late 1800s. The first pioneer settlers came to Nayoro in the year 1900 where there was an Aboriginal Ainu village. It was proposed that we consider an appointment to the town of Nayoro. This proved to be a good choice, since we remained there till 1981, for the rest of our missionary service in Japan.

THE BIG MOVE TO HOKKAIDO

It was an exciting time preparing for our move from Tokyo to Hokkaido in the fall of 1953. In consultation with Alf Stone and the Nayoro church it was decided that the mission board would build a house for us. Church members negotiated for a three lot plot of land at the north end of town. This would give room for a playground and a large garden plot. The building contract was given to a local contractor with supervision by a Sapporo architectural firm, since this was the first "western style" home to be built in Nayoro.

The expectation was that the house was to be finished by October. However, we were ready to move by the end of August. Alf Stone suggested that even though the house might not be finished, if a second storey were built on the garage, we could camp there and supervise the building of the house until we moved in. The request was made that the garage be completed first so that we could move there by the end of August.

We left Tokyo on August 25th, 1953, this time travelling north by train, stopping off with the MacLeods in Otaru to celebrate the first birthdays of Dennis and Patsy. We arrived in Nayoro on August 29th to find the garage only partially completed. The large garage doors were not yet in place and there were no toilet facilities. We packed our many boxes and trunks at one end of the garage shutting out the view from the street, and used the second storey for sleeping quarters. We had a kerosene range for cooking and in a few days a privy was attached and a small wood stove installed. Running water from the pump in the basement of the house was hooked up with one tap, and a tin sink with a drain hose through the wall to the back of the garage.

Washing clothes called for some creative innovation. We did have an electric washing machine with a ringer. Water was heated on the kerosene range. We set a large metal wash tub on the top of a small kitchen step ladder and filled the tub with cold water for rinsing. One day when we were doing the washing Dennis was trying to help by standing on one step of the ladder and pulling on the clothes as they came out of the ringer. All of a sudden the tub of cold water tipped on top of Dennis which prompted a huge shriek, but he was none the worse for his ordeal. Doreen found these first few months living in the garage, a difficult time. Every time she stepped outside she felt uneasy when the workmen stared at her out of curiosity.

Two years of language study meant that by this time we were partially fluent in Japanese. We could do our own shopping and carry on simple conversations. The neighbours were most friendly and helpful. Our closest neighbours were the Kurisu family who had a dairy farm. Shortly after we arrived, Mr. Kurisu appeared on the steps leading to our second storey "apartment" with the gift of a steaming bowl of field corn.

Unfortunately, the contractor was unable to meet the October date for the completion of the house and we were not able to move into the house until December 5th. By this time there was snow on the ground and the inside of the cement walls of the garage were covered with frost. When we moved into the house, the kitchen counters and linoleum flooring were not yet installed but we moved anyway.

About a month after our arrival we received a telegram telling us that my father had died. We knew that he had terminal cancer but it was impossible to return even for his funeral. In going to Japan we had always realised this was one of the personal sacrifices we would have to make. We had to satisfy ourselves with a "wire-recorder" audio-tape of the memorial service, sent by my brother Maurice. The Nayoro church elders brought flowers and shared in our grief.

While we were still living in the garage Ian and Virginia MacLeod paid us a visit and shared our humble abode for one night. We divided the upstairs room of the garage into a "two bedroom apartment" with a curtain down the middle. Their visit rescued us from loneliness and helped us discover the humour in our living situation.

We were the first "foreign family" to live in the area and became the greatest curiosity in the countryside. When we went into town to shop, the children crowded around, crawling up on the sides of the Jeep, peeking in every window to get a better look at Dennis. Dennis smiled and babbled to the children, but his parents found the attention disconcerting. On another occasion, when we went to visit an orphanage in the neighbouring town of Bifuka, while I was inside the building meeting the staff, most of the children in the orphanage crowded around the Jeep where Doreen and Dennis sat. Doreen almost panicked, and after I came out, we went down the road, stopped, and talked over the trauma she had experienced.

SETTLING INTO OUR NEW HOME
Our western style house attracted a great deal of attention. The basic plan was patterned on the pre-fab house which had been shipped to Tokyo from British Columbia for the Stones. We made some improvements to the plan based on our experience of living in the Tokyo house for almost two years. The Hokkaido architect advised a hip roof to deal with the excessive snow for which Nayoro was famous. We appreciated this when we found that snow piled up so high that it blocked the windows until it was shovelled away. The hip roof also provided more spacious upstairs rooms and ample storage space

By February, the inside work had been completed so we decided to have an "open-house" for church members. However, Mr. Tamura, who was very proud of our new house, put a notice in the paper inviting the whole town. Fortunately for us, there was a big storm that day and only about 50 people turned up. Everyone wanted a tour of the house from basement to second storey. Later, in the summer, we found that whole busloads of people were asking to see through the house. By this time we were feeling overwhelmed by all the attention. Some people from the countryside who had never seen a bed before enjoyed sitting or bouncing on the bed. When we discovered that Mr. Tamura had put the house on the city hall list of interesting sights in Nayoro we politely objected and had it taken off the list.

Years later, when I was getting a haircut from my barber, a church elder, Mr. Wakayama, mentioned that we had a great influence on the people of Nayoro. Hoping to hear that it had been my sermons or work in the community he told me that life had been transformed for the housewives of Nayoro, who after seeing our modern kitchen, hounded their husbands until they got one too. The kitchen in the traditional Japanese home was a dingy inconvenient room at the back of the house. Almost all new homes from that time on were built with modern, more convenient kitchens.

The Japanese heating methods were completely inadequate for our house. Most homes had one small stove set in the middle of their living rooms burning coal, wood or sawdust.

Other rooms were usually unheated. In the winter they filled a crockery "hot water bottle" to warm their "futon" bedding. During our stay in Nayoro our heating system went through a number of transformations. When the house was being built we had a coal burning furnace sent from Vancouver and had duct work installed so that the whole house could be heated. This was effective for heating the house but we had a few bad experiences with the available soft coal exploding and filling the house with smoke.

We next decided to experiment with saw-dust heat. Nayoro was a lumber town with lots of cheap excess saw-dust. I heard that sawdust was used extensively for heating in British Columbia, so on our first home assignment in 1956-57 we stopped in Vancouver and talked to the company that had provided the coal furnace. The manager told me that he did have a sawdust burner that could be attached to our furnace. This attachment would be given free. All the Mission Board would have to do was to pay the shipping. When the saw-dust burner arrived we fastened it to the furnace and filled the coal bin and all free space under the house with sawdust. The sawdust provided a steady warm heat. The only draw-back was that the huge saw-dust bin in the front of the furnace had to be filled twice a day using buckets by pouring the saw-dust into the top of the hopper. I did not find this much of a chore, but since I was often away from home, the task fell to Doreen more than she appreciated. In addition, when the furnace went out it took a genius to get it started again. I had mastered the technique, but Doreen had not. One time when I was away Doreen had a missionary friend staying with her. They forgot to fill up the bin, the furnace went out, and they had to spend most of an evening trying to get it started.

Finally, after a number of years, when furnace oil had become available in Nayoro, we asked if we could have an oil furnace shipped over. The Mission Board graciously agreed to our request. This was much more convenient, since it was run with a thermostat. The only difficulty was that there was no one in Nayoro qualified to service the furnace. This was an art I had to learn myself. I became quite proficient at cleaning the furnace and trouble shooting when it refused to function properly.

CHURCH ACTIVITIES

Beginning work in a new land with different customs and language had its special challenges. We learned to use many new foods, since most western type foods were not available. One day we thought we had made a great discovery when we found a store that stocked sealed cans of oatmeal. There was one bakery, but it sold only white bread and sweet buns filled with bean curd, not our favourite. The stores did have excellent cod and salmon. We especially relished the communal feasts around a charcoal burner with a clay pot on top containing fish and many types of vegetables from which everyone ate. The most delicious feast, and most expensive, was the beef sukiyaki meal. It wasn't long till our daily menu was a mixture of Japanese and western style dishes.

No one in Nayoro could really speak English. Even the gracious Mrs. Ishida, a high school English teacher who became our Japanese language teacher, did not have the self confidence to engage in English conversation. Mrs. Ishida was a war widow whose husband had been killed in the war serving in the Japanese army. She lived with her doctor brother and his wife and was the head of the English department in the Nayoro high school. She became a close personal friend as well as our teacher.

Mrs. Ishida came to our house several times a week to teach us lessons from our Japanese language text book and to help me translate sermons from English into Japanese. An incident occurred when preaching one of my early sermons in the Nayoro church in February of 1954, the same weekend as our "open house." With Mrs. Ishida's help I had carefully prepared a manuscript which I had practised reading. As I was preaching the sermon on Sunday I suddenly discovered that the last page of my manuscript was missing. When the guests had come the day before I had tucked the sermon in a desk drawer and missed taking out the last page. I was at a complete loss. I could not continue without a manuscript. I turned to the minister, Mr.

Tamura, for help. Without missing a beat he picked up where I had left off with what he thought might be an appropriate ending for my sermon.

Mr. Tamura had worked out a busy schedule for us almost as soon as we arrived. Frequently I was asked to preach at the Sunday worship in the Nayoro church that had about sixty members. There were morning and evening church services on Sunday and a Wednesday night Bible study and prayer service. He had also started meetings in several surrounding towns. The main task he gave me was to assist in meetings in the surrounding towns and villages. In Shimokawa, a village about fifteen kilometres east, he had started to build a little church, that for a time was called the smallest church in Japan. I was there in time to help drive some of the last nails into this structure. It had no chairs or pews, so the congregation sat on the floor. There were only seven members. Meetings were held in the church even before it was completed and I was given the honour of preaching the first sermon. That evening, with many members from the Nayoro church, about 60 people crowded into the tiny space. From then on Mr. Tamura and I took turns holding services there on Sunday evenings. Sometimes I would load eight or nine young people from Nayoro into the Jeep to assist in the service and the singing.

In addition, Mr. Tamura asked me to accompany him to the occasional "house meeting" in the town of Shibetsu and villages of Wassamu and Furen. Before long I was taking charge of these by myself. Several times during the winter I took the three hour train trip to Wakkanai, at the northern tip of Japan, to assist Miss Hatanaka, the deaconess in charge of the little church there. Miss Hatanaka was an enthusiastic middle aged woman who had been sent to Wakkanai to revive a church that had faded out during the war years. An earnest group of Christians gathered every Sunday and there was a thriving Sunday School. When I went to Wakkanai I preached the sermon and sometimes led a communion service and performed baptismal ceremonies.

Christmas, for Mr. Tamura, was a big opportunity for community children's meetings. One of these that I remember in particular, was in the mountain village of Shumarinai. There was one Christian disabled man in this village whom we visited from time to time. At Christmas, with his help, a large hall was reserved and an invitation sent out to all the children in the village to come to a Christmas party. I think most of the children in the village attended. We had a program of Christmas songs, telling Christmas stories using "kamishibai" story telling placards. We also had Christmas gifts for everyone. In some of these communities we followed up with after school children's meetings once a month.

In May of 1954 we put our house facilities to good use with a leadership training weekend for Christian youth in the northern area. About sixteen young people stayed for two nights and Nayoro young people commuted from their homes. With the assistance of Don Clugston, Mr. Tamura, and Miss Hatanaka, courses were given on methods of Bible study, teaching children, worship leadership and planning young peoples' programmes. This along with a Rural Gospel School held in the house were our first experiments in the feasibility of a conference centre for the northern Hokkaido region, that was realized when we built the Northern Hokkaido Christian Centre in 1960.

RURAL GOSPEL SCHOOLS
Rural Gospel Schools in Japan had a long history with schools on the main island of Honshu dating back to 1927 under the Rev. Toyohiko Kagawa and other Japanese rural education leaders. In 1929 Alfred Stone, building on earlier work of Kagawa, held the first rural gospel school in Niigata. The curriculum for these schools somewhat resembled scaled down versions of theological schools with courses on the Bible, Christian education, and Christian faith as well as topics like rural sociology, rural economics, state ideology, and discussion of other religions. These were held for about one week.

Our first attempts at a rural gospel school in Hokkaido were much more modest, one or two day events. Alf Stone, one of the leaders of the 1929 Honshu schools, helped us plan ours. Mr. Tamura and I arranged two series of Rural Gospel Schools in January and March of 1954. The meetings were usually held in community halls. The first of the one day schools was held in Shimokawa, the village where the new church had been built. This was followed by schools in Nayoro, in the rural church in Nakagawa, one and one half hours by train north of Nayoro, and the village of Otoineppu where we had no church contacts at all. Publicity for these events was carried out through the Rural Agricultural Cooperatives that exist in every town. In the most rural areas, where there was no regular telephone service, farmers had put up their own one line telephone lines. At several set times each day announcements of upcoming events were made and everyone on line was expected to "tune in." We were able to make use of this service for our publicity.

At each of the schools we had an attendance of forty to sixty farm people. They were particularly interested because they knew of the work of Toyohiko Kagawa. The fact that two co-workers of Kagawa, missionary Alf Stone and Rev. Toshi Kimata, would be speakers no doubt sparked their interest. They were especially impressed by the fact that Alf Stone could speak to them humourously in colloquial Japanese. His message was related to the issue of the hardships farmers were facing in the post-war era, and the need for some kind of faith to overcome the challenges. He did not try to foist Christianity on them but did let it be known that for himself he was speaking out of a Christian perspective. Toshi Kimata, who was a rural sociologist as well as a minister, spoke of the sociological basis of Japanese rural society with suggestions of ways in which they could organize their communities to be more mutually supportive and effective. I gave a talk on rural life in Canada telling about my own farm life and the importance of Christianity on farm and community life. For the March series we again had the help of Alf Stone along with a new Canadian missionary, the Rev. Don Orth, a graduate of Guelph Agricultural College and Emmanuel Theological College. He had recently been stationed in Obihiro in the southern part of Hokkaido.

One of the schools was again held for a two day period in our house in Nayoro. The women of the church made straw mattress "futon" which were spread out for sleeping in the upper rooms of the house and in the top floor of the garage. We also purchased blankets. In this way twenty people were able to crowd in for overnight accommodation, in addition to others who commuted from their homes.

These schools proved to be particularly helpful in the post-war era for farm youth who were becoming discontented with farm life and who were looking for a new purpose. Alf Stone's talks on the connection between faith and life particularly caught their attention. One young farmer wrote to me afterwards: "I have determined to use all my power in using the knowledge I gained at the Gospel School in building a brighter farm life and better village life."

SUMMER TENT CARAVANS

A unique outreach into new communities was one pioneered by a U.S. Methodist missionary, Evyn Adams, in rural districts around Sapporo. This involved the participation of university students in summer caravans holding meetings in a large portable tent in communities in which there was no church. In the summer of 1954 we decided to adapt this approach with some of the communities in northern Hokkaido. The first Caravan was made up of four university students from Tokyo, two theological students on summer church appointments, Lloyd Graham, Mr. Tamura and myself. We purchased a large tent that we transported by trailer pulled behind our Jeep. We went to five towns and villages, spending three or four days in each place. For these communities it was like a summer circus coming to town. We had no trouble gathering a crowd. We had a programme for children in the afternoons and another for young people and adults in the evening. The children's programme consisted of songs, Bible stories, marionettes, slides and movies. In some villages 400 to 500 children would jam into the tent. In the evenings we showed a general interest film on Canada and then a Bible story film in Japanese. One student would talk about what the Christian faith had come to mean to him or her, followed by small group discussions.

Mr. Tagashira, a student from the International Christian University, had a particularly moving story. His family had been living in the heart of Hiroshima where his father was a Japanese Methodist minister. On August 6th, 1945, the day the atom bomb was dropped on Hiroshima, he had just arrived at his school in a suburb when he heard a tremendous explosion and saw the mushroom cloud billow over Hiroshima. He himself was far enough away that he was not affected. However, days later when it was safe for him to go into the city he discovered that his home had been destroyed and there was no trace of his father and mother. A great sense of despair came over him; he wondered if life was worth living. However, in the ruins of his home he found his father's Bible. He read the words in the 23rd Psalm, "The Lord is my shepherd, I shall not want." He realized then, that he was not alone, that God was with him. He said that although nothing was left of his material possessions, the most precious gift was the one his parents had already given him, the gift of a Christian faith, and this gift he now wanted to pass on to others.

One of the particularly memorable meetings was in Okoppe, a rural community on the east coast. In the other communities we usually had a Christian family or two who were key contacts. They would often billet the caravan members and help with publicity and arrangements. In Okoppe there were no Christian contacts. However, we put up the tent in an open space in front of the railway station. At the end of the first evening meeting, a young school teacher came to us and said that she and her family were Christian. The next day we drove out to the Sato farm home where we met her mother and four other children. The mother could hardly contain her joy. She said that she and her husband who were both Christians, had moved there twenty-three years previously. Her husband had been killed by a bull and she had raised the children as Christians by herself, reading the Bible with them and singing hymns. In all of those twenty three years we were the first Christian contacts they had. We began to wonder how our Christianity would have survived if we had been kept in similar isolation from the fellowship of other Christians. The Sato family became the core of a new Christian group in Okoppe which grew out of that caravan. For several years Mr. Tamura and I took turns, each holding a meeting in the community hall once a month. The Sato family were joined by quite a few of the high school students who had attended the caravan meetings.

A few years later, the Rev. Ishikawa and his wife were sent to Okoppe and together with the help of the Sato family and a few new members were able to build a small church and kindergarten. The church was partly financed from kindergarten revenue, with the rest coming from the Hokkaido district Pioneer Evangelism Fund. Financing small churches by running a kindergarten is a common practice in Japan. Although most of the parents are not Christian, they appreciate the moral education these kindergartens provide.

Caravans were carried on for four consecutive summers, visiting a total of eleven different communities, some of them several times. As a result of this outreach ministry two new churches were established and six "house churches" in peoples' homes were formed. I made monthly visits by train and Jeep to each of the house churches, again taking turns with Mr. Tamura or one of the new Japanese ministers.

Initially, before the advent of television, large crowds gathered, but gradually curiosity waned and the caravans were discontinued. However, we felt that, especially among the young people, they had served a purpose. Some who had faced real disillusionment about the war found a whole new meaning for life. These young people formed seekers groups to study the Bible together and often became the core of the new churches. One high school student said that he had always thought that religion was for "long-faced" people, but that he had been impressed by the cheerfulness of the caravaners and he wanted to discover what they had found.

HOKKAIDO PIONEER EVANGELISM PROGRAM

Shortly before we went to Hokkaido, the Hokkaido District of the United Church of Christ in Japan developed a plan for mission outreach called the Pioneer Evangelism Program. One goal of this plan was to more than double the number of United

Church of Christ churches in Hokkaido within ten years. They proposed a five year plan. Christian groups who wanted a church were given assistance to build a church and to support a minister. A major part of the funds for this outreach program came from overseas churches in the United States and Canada through the Interboard Committee for Christian Work in Japan. These new churches were expected to become self-supporting within a five year period. Under this plan a number of Christian groups that came together in various communities throughout Hokkaido obtained the assistance of a minister and funds to build a church.

In the northern Hokkaido district, in which we were working, churches were built in Shimokawa, Wassamu, Shibetsu and Okoppe. Throughout Hokkaido under the Pioneer Evangelism Plan the number of new churches more than doubled from about 25 to about 60 within 25 years. This gave us considerable encouragement in the work we were doing. Not until after the first eight years did we try to challenge the church on its traditional pattern of being closed communities with little relationship to the world around them. We cooperated with them in carrying out what they saw as their mission, that of forming more Christian communities and building new churches. The opportunity of working towards community-centred church programmes and structures did not present itself until after the building of the Northern Hokkaido Christian Centre in 1960 and I was joined as Co-director of the Centre by Rev. Mitsuo Nakamura, trainee of the pioneer social activist the Rev. Toyohiko Kagawa.

FROM BARN TO CHURCH

This is a story of the birth of a pioneer church in the village of Wassamu nestled in a lovely valley about half way between Nayoro and Asahigawa. About forty years prior to our arrival, a Christian farmer by the name of Nagumo had come to the area and carved a farm out of the wilderness. Not many years later Mr. Nagumo was killed by a bear, leaving his wife to raise a large family. Even though there was no church in the village, the children were raised as Christians and the eldest son, who inherited the farm, eventually became mayor of the village. His father had established the first dairy farm in the district and the son had turned this into a thriving dairy business producing, processing and distributing milk to the village.

With the Nagumo family's help, one of the rural gospel schools, a forerunner of our later Three Love Schools, was held in Wassamu. About forty farmers and their wives attended the school and showed an interest, not only in the agricultural aspects of the program but in the Christian message as well. The following summer a three day tent caravan went to the village and a theological student from Kyoto was placed in Wassamu for the summer months to hold weekly Sunday services and to visit homes in the community. The work was further strengthened by the arrival of a graduate of the Nopporo Christian Agricultural College, Mr. Takahashi, himself an enthusiastic Christian. He started a poultry farm and became leader of the 4-H Club (a cooperative youth organization), many of whose members also began attending church. After the theological student left, Mr. Tamura and I each went to Wassamu for house meetings in the Nagumo home. The attendance grew to about fifteen people and they started talking about building a church.

Mr. Nagumo made available an old barn, which had been used as a milk receiving station, and also donated some land on a corner of his property. Application was made to the United Church of Japan District Executive to be included under the Pioneer Evangelism Plan. In April of 1955 their new minister, Rev. Jo Kamatani and his wife, Michiko, arrived from Kyoto, where Jo had just graduated from the Doshisha Theological Seminary. For several months they lived in rented rooms until the church could be built. The barn was moved to the property and completely rebuilt with a sanctuary on the lower level and rooms for the Kamatanis on the second storey. In the same summer another tent Caravan visited Wassamu and on a Sunday morning the first church service was held in the partially completed church. The chancel was not yet boarded in, but as we looked out through the open wall to the hills beyond we gave thanks for the little group who, because a stable was not too humble for the birth of Jesus, had the vision of turning a barn into a lovely little church.

The Kamatanis remained in Wassamu for five years, giving leadership not only in ministry in the church but in service to the rural community and youth groups. Two sons were born to them in Wassamu. Doreen and I visited them frequently, and we became especially close friends. After leaving Wassamu, the Kamatanis returned to Kyoto where Jo eventually became the Principal of the High School division of Doshisha University. It was found that in small rural villages like Wassamu, the hope of the Pioneer Evangelism Plan of becoming financially independent in five years was impractical. Although each year a few more young people would join the church, on graduation from high school they would almost all move away. The result was that the number of members living in Wassamu never seemed to grow beyond the original number of fifteen. However, in a few years another pioneer church had been established in the nearby city of Shibetsu and, with a minister appointed there, Shibetsu and Wassamu were formed into a two church pastoral charge with the minister living in the larger town of Shibetsu.

An interesting sequel to the story of the barn that became a church took place about fifteen years later when the building was destroyed by fire. A young man who had attended a youth group in the church when he was a high school student, had moved away with his family. However, he became despondent. He came back to Wassamu, and decided to commit suicide in the church by setting fire to himself in front of the pulpit. He started the fire, but then fled. The members of congregation were very sorry to lose their church, but they were even more concerned about the young man. They got in touch with him and his family and let them know that they would not be laying charges, and that they would like to help him in any way they could. They decided to rebuild the church. Funds were raised by churches throughout Japan and they built a more beautiful church than they had before.

ALFRED STONE: MENTOR AND FRIEND

In many ways the mantle of Alf Stone seemed to fall on us from the time we arrived in Japan. Although he and Jean and their two boys, Donald and Robert, had left Japan on home-assignment before we arrived in September of 1951, we inherited the mission house in which they had been living, the Jeep which he had been using, and we also inherited some of the vision and the work of rural mission outreach that was his greatest passion. We didn't actually meet Alf until he arrived back in Tokyo in the fall of 1953, having left Jean with the boys in Canada to continue their education. We saw him frequently while we were still in Tokyo. He shared with us his vision of a rebuilt Japan and of his desire to again promote mission outreach among the rural population of Japan. Alf was happy to hear that we were interested in working in rural Hokkaido and was instrumental in getting us posted to Nayoro. He accompanied us on our first trip to Nayoro and helped us plan the building of the Nayoro house and to supervise it when it was under construction. In the fall of 1954 he moved to Sapporo to undertake rural mission work in Hokkaido himself and to be a support to ourselves and the other new Canadian missionaries working in Hokkaido. He made a special trip to visit us in Nayoro just a few days before going on a fateful journey back to Honshu aboard the ill-fated ferry boat the Toyamaru.

THE TRAGEDY OF THE SINKING OF THE TOYAMARU

Since Doreen and I were associated closely with the tragedy of the Toyamaru I will try to reconstruct what happened from my own experience and memory. A Council of Cooperation Conference of the Kyodan had been called for September 28th, 1954 at Karuizawa, west of Tokyo. All Kyodan related missionaries in Japan were asked to attend. Doreen and I and two-year-old Dennis made plans to travel to Honshu. We had received word from my mother that she was coming to Japan to spend some time with us. Since her arrival date was just one week before the conference we decided to leave early. Doreen and Dennis went to stay with the Bascoms in Hirosaki in northern Honshu, and I went on to meet mother in Tokyo. Mother and I spent a few days in Tokyo and the resort town of Nikko and then I took her to Nagano to visit the home of another Canadian missionary family, the Carey's, before I went on to the Karuizawa conference.

While still in Tokyo we heard that there had been a terrible typhoon in northern Japan. When we arrived in Nagano we got the news of the sinking of the Toyamaru ferry boat. In the evening we heard that although the Canadian missionary, Don Orth, had been saved, Alf Stone and Dean Leeper, a YMCA worker, had lost their lives. In a diary that mother kept she wrote:

> If I hadn't come to Japan, Floyd and Doreen would likely have been on that same ferry. God moves in a mysterious way. Alf Stone was like a father to all the younger missionaries.

After attending the conference we started back to Hokkaido. The sea was peaceful as we came into the Hakodate harbour, but there was devastation all around. About a dozen ships of varying sizes were overturned in the harbour. The largest was the Toyamaru. We were met by Isabel Leith, a Canadian missionary living in Hakodate, who took us to her home where Don Orth was recovering from his ordeal. We had planned on taking Don home with us immediately, but since he was still recovering from a wound on his head and fatigue, we stayed on for several days and attended the Sunday service in the Hakodate Church and heard in the sermon of the minister, Rev Nobuo Kusama more details about the tragedy of the previous Sunday.

Rev. Kusama had asked Alf to preach at the church service the previous Sunday. After the service Alf had left his black gown with Mr. Kusama and had gone down to board the ferry. There had been several delays during which more and more people boarded the Toyamaru from incoming trains. The Toyamaru was a huge ferry with cars, trucks, and railway box cars on the lower deck, making it very unwieldy. The storm had already hit before the ferry took off, but during a lull, which proved to be the eye of the storm, the ferry pulled into the harbour. Before the ferry had cleared the harbour it was hit by 140 kilometre per hour winds. Even though it put down an anchor it was blown back into the harbour and overturned. A total of 1,055 people lost their lives and only 159 were saved. It was a tragedy second only to the sinking of the Titanic in scale.

The Rev. Kusama, wearing Alf's gown for the service, remarked that he had the sense of being Elisha wearing the mantle of Elijah. Elisha had been named the successor of Elijah in an Old Testament story when Elijah had been taken up to the heavens. In his sermon Rev. Kusama told a story he had heard from a Teachers' College student, one of the survivors of the Toyamaru catastrophe. I have a translated copy of the sermon, sent to me later by Isabel Leith. This is the story as told by the Rev. Kusama:

> The student was on the same boat, Toyamaru, with Rev. Stone. When the water began to dash into the ferry Rev. Stone was helping those students put on life belts. The boat was sinking. One of the students asked Rev. Stone to put one on himself, "Reverend, why don't you have one? We are in great danger. The boat will sink in a moment." To this Rev. Stone replied, "Young man, I have come to Japan to die for her; I am rather old but you are still young. You have to live longer and work for Japan. Come quick." Then he even gave the life belt which he had for his own use to another student. "I will be praying for you all", he shouted, "so that you can be rescued." Those students swam out of that sinking boat with Rev. Stone praying aloud for them . . . Isn't this the very spirit that has sent missionaries to Japan? Isn't this the very power that has made Christianity a world-wide religion. . . Surely he was the incarnation of the spirit of Christ. . . I pay anew my deepest respect and love to him as one of the greatest missionaries who did live both in his life and death the words of Jesus, "Greater love has no man than this, that a man lay down his life for his friends."

This account struck us deeply and filled our hearts with a great sense of sorrow and loss. The story of Alf's self sacrifice was spread all over Japan and the memory of it remains alive in Japan to this day. We took Don Orth home with us to Nayoro to recover from cuts and bruises and from the trauma of the whole experience. Don stayed with us a week before returning to work in Obihiro in southern Hokkaido. He was a graduate of the Ontario Agricultural College in Guelph before going to Emmanuel College to train for the ministry. Because of his agricultural training he was later transferred to the Rural Theological Seminary in Tsurukawa, south of Tokyo, as director of its farming operations and teacher of practical agriculture to the theological students. The Rural Theological Seminary was the successor to a National Christian Rural Service and Training Centre, which Alf Stone had helped to establish at Hino, a suburb of Tokyo. The main building of the new theological Centre was appropriately named, "The A.R. Stone Memorial Building."

ALF STONE'S LIFE AND VISION

Alf Stone and I came from different generations, but it is remarkable the way we shared many of the same values and faith perspectives. Considering the influence that Alf had on both my rural mission in Hokkaido, and on my faith perspective, I think it is valuable to tell some of Alf's life story. Fortunately, I can draw on both recollections of Alf himself and from the biography of his life, *Requiem From The Sea*, written by Kunji Niihori and translated by Rob Witmer.

Alf was born on a farm near Highgate in western Ontario in 1902. He studied Arts and Theology at Victoria College, Toronto, where he also took courses in Agricultural Economics. He was sent to Japan in 1926 as a missionary of the newly formed United Church of Canada. For two years he studied the Japanese language and soon became quite fluent. After five years as a single missionary, he married Jean Gillespie, a United Church missionary who had preceded him by one year. Jean had worked as an English teacher and principal of a church kindergarten. They were married in her home church in Parry Sound in 1931 on their first home assignment.

Alf was introduced to rural evangelism by the pioneer Canadian missionary Daniel Norman when he was sent to work with him in the Nagano region. Kuniji Niihori remarks, "rural evangelism was the greatest legacy which Norman was to leave Stone." He also records that when Stone presented a Bible to a graduate of a Rural Gospel School Alf wrote inside the cover, "I love God, I love humanity, I love the soil."

Alf and Jean returned to Japan together in 1932 and were assigned to new work in Hamamatsu in Shizuoka Prefecture developing Rural Gospel Schools and establishing rural church kindergartens. In 1934 they were transferred to Nagano where he gradually took over the work of Daniel Norman, then in his seventies. In his new role Alf expanded the work to develop a "rural parish" - a new concept, much more in keeping with what is now considered a "modern" development approach. Alf's parish plan included an attempt to meet not only the spiritual needs of people associated with the church, but also the physical needs of the impoverished communities. He helped to expand a small forge which manufactured sickles; he assisted in the formation of a vegetable co-op and a marketing system to facilitate sales of canned produce and a "friendship fund" credit union.

Alf subscribed to a theology of "personal salvation," broadened by a "social gospel," seeking to create a just society. Sharing this same basic creed, Alf and his fellow Christians in the Nagano district worked to bring about effective and significant change in rural society as a whole.

PEACE AND WAR

Alf and I shared similar philosophies with regard to peace and war. His principles were put to the test during the Japanese invasion of China in the thirties. A National Mobilization Act was passed by the Japanese government and all religious groups were brought under the National Unification Plan. Many of the youth with whom the church had been working were conscripted into the army. Foreigners were under suspicion by the government. Even missionaries' sermons were monitored for "unpatriotic" sentiments. Alf became aware that he was being followed by military police and was questioned on numerous occasions. Alf had to be very careful about what he said in public, but he still continued to speak to his Christian friends about peace. In a confidential letter sent to Canada he wrote:

> This is not the holy war the Japanese government makes it out to be. The genocide being carried out against the Chinese people is unforgivable. Japanese militarism and totalitarianism snatches the future from the young men here and endangers the entire country.

Alf's movements within Japan became more and more restricted and even Japanese people who associated with him were in danger of being harassed by the police. Rural evangelism became impossible. He had to give up the work in Nagano and moved to Tokyo as movement by foreigners was being restricted. Alf left Japan in March of 1941 for Canada. His wife and family had preceded him previously.

The war years were spent as the minister of the Appin charge in south-western Ontario. In Canada he criticized the government for their evacuation of Japanese Canadians from the west coast and he befriended some of the evacuees who had been brought to a neighbouring town to work in the sugar beet fields. Alf returned to a defeated Japan in October of 1946, and immediately threw himself into repairing some of the damage caused by the war. Working with the United Church of Christ in Japan he helped to gather together scattered Christians, repossessing church property and rebuilding churches, especially in the rural areas. He helped to re-establish Rural Gospel Schools and assisted in implementing a Rural Evangelism Committee in Hokkaido. One of his dreams that was realized was the founding of the National Christian Rural Service and Training Centre for the training of rural evangelists in Hino, a suburb of Tokyo. Alf Stone was the first Principal and taught a course on Rural Sociology.

Alf was fully prepared to support the action of the United Church of Christ in Japan (Kyodan) in their March 1954 protest against the United States test of the hydrogen bomb in the Bikini atoll. Several Japanese fishermen were caught in the fallout. The Japanese population were greatly incensed by this action. Alf Stone, along with other missionaries working in Japan, wrote a strong letter to the U.S. churches, stating in part:

> The church must not compromise itself. It must at all times speak out prophetically against evil . . . we missionaries join with the Kyodan in praying from the bottom of our hearts that God may use this open letter to put an end to all testing of atomic weapons, and guide us in such a way that their production will be banned.

Peace, not only for Japan but for the whole world, became one of Alf's passions in life. He became a role model for me in working against the re-militarization of Japan. I joined in the Japanese attempts to protect the peace constitution and to protest the actions of the right wing government glorifying the war and building up Japan's military strength. A Japanese army base, that the government named "the Japanese Self Defence Force" was established in Nayoro. The Dohoku Centre, of which I was the Director, in cooperation with the Nayoro church, organized twice yearly community wide events to protest government action and to carry out peace education among the citizens.

LIFE IN NAYORO WITH MOTHER HOWLETT

After my father died in the fall of 1953, we urged mother to come and live with us. What finally convinced her that she was needed was when we announced that another baby was on the way. With her nursing training she would be an invaluable help. All her life she had been interested in overseas mission. She had been an active member of the United Church Women's Missionary Society in which she diligently studied the work of the church overseas. To be able to see mission being carried out first-hand was a further incentive to her making the trip.

To her consternation, in Nayoro, she soon realized that we were the only people with whom she could communicate. She was not completely isolated however. We visited back and forth with the Clugstons in Asahigawa. She attended the annual inter-church Hokkaido Missionary Fellowship and also joined us on the long trek to Tokyo for two spring meetings of the all-Japan Kyodan Related Missionary Conference. She enjoyed accompanying us to the churches in Shimokawa, Okoppe, Wassamu, Wakkanai and house meetings in northern Hokkaido. After attending one of her first church services in the Nayoro church she recorded in her diary:

> Floyd and I went to church. Mr. Tamura preached. I couldn't understand, but I enjoyed the spirit of worship and the fellowship. I think I can feel nearer to God when I don't understand the minister. I can pray and commune with God all the time and it makes the time pass very peacefully and beautifully. It is wonderful to know that God understands both languages and that we are all one in Christ Jesus.

Mother was a great help with the cooking classes in our home. She also taught English to a few students. My schedule became busier than ever in my second year and I often had to be away overnight. I was happy that mother could be with Doreen, particularly as the time for the birth of the baby drew near. Doreen would go to Sapporo for the birth, attended by an Australian woman missionary physician, Dr. Ormiston, who lived in Sapporo. We had arranged to have the birth in the Catholic hospital with Dr. Ormiston in charge. Since the hospital was run by Japanese nuns, we of course obtained their agreement to the arrangement. They kept it a secret from the Japanese doctor who usually attended births, that a foreign doctor was in charge of the delivery.

On March 14th we all went to Sapporo and stayed with Mildred Brown, a missionary teacher friend at the Hokusei Girls' High School. While there we went to the station to say goodbye to Ruth Clugston and her new baby, John, who were returning to Asahigawa. We boarded the train to say goodbye and didn't hear the bell announcing the train's departure. We all rushed off in time, but by the time Doreen got to the door the train was already moving. Millie Brown ran alongside the train and caught Doreen's hand as she jumped. This episode may have brought on the birth of our second baby.

That same night at 2 a.m. Doreen and I went to the hospital by taxi. Millie continued on in the same taxi to pick up Dr. Ormiston. First of all they had trouble finding the doctor's residence and then the taxi got stuck in the snow. Doctor Ormiston got there just in time for the baby to be born at 5 a.m. on March 17th. We named him Peter. Mother and I returned to Nayoro and a week later I went again by train to Sapporo to bring Doreen and Peter home. When we arrived back in Nayoro our road was blocked with snow, so our neighbour Mr. Kurisu transported us the last part of the journey in his one horse open sleigh. Dennis was happy to have a baby brother.

Mother was with us for about 20 months and, for both Doreen and myself, was a great source of spiritual strength. She was interested in the work we were doing, and won the hearts of the many people who came to know her. In her Christmas 1955 newsletter to friends back in Canada, she wrote more about her activities in Japan:

> It has been so nice to be with Floyd and Doreen and my dear grandchildren, Dennis and Peter. Since I have been with Peter ever since he was born, I almost feel as if he were my own baby. He is such a darling. Dennis is a live wire - nothing slow about him. I have had a wonderful year with new experiences and customs every day. Some of them, such as sitting on the floor and sleeping on the floor on futon (padded quilts), I find rather hard for an old lady who is not used to it. But I manage not too badly. I can eat my bowl of rice with chop sticks, not quite as easily as they do, but I manage to clean out my bowl. However these customs are only put into practice when we go away from home, as we live in a western style house, much the same as we do in Canada.

> What a barrier this language is. So often I would like to tell some one the wonderful Good News about Jesus but can't make myself understood. So all I can hope to do is to relieve Floyd and Doreen as much as I can so they can do what I would like to do. Floyd's house is right out in the farming district and I enjoy watching the different ways of doing things. All the work is done by hand. The grain is cut with a little sickle and hung up on a trellis to dry and flailed out when dry. Only one family next to us is more modern in their farming. They have cows and a silo and they fill their silo much as we do at home.

Her witness was not so much in words as in her presence and her love and concern for all the people she met. By the time she left I feel sure she had in a sense fulfilled her dream of being a missionary overseas.

MOTHER'S LIFE OF SERVICE IN CANADA

Mother returned to Canada with us when we left Japan for our first home assignment in June of 1956. Within a short time she had sold her home in Elora and moved into the Hidden Springs Centre, a half way house for people with mental illness and recovering alcoholics, that my brother Ralph had established near Paris, Ontario. Mother was the house mother for the men's residence. Her complete acceptance of each individual and her loving support was a healing presence for all who came. This was another valuable mission mother was able to fulfil, this time in Canada. She stayed there for about ten years, after which she finally "retired" to a small house in Guelph. She died there in January of 1971 at the age of 83. I was always sorry that I couldn't be with her at the last. She knew she had a terminal illness but insisted that we had said our good-byes the year before, when we were back in Canada, and that I should not leave Doreen and the children alone in the house in the dead of winter. Mother's self-giving love was a model that I can never forget.

Hilda Howlett in Japan with Doreen and Floyd

Open house in Nayoro

Dohoku Christian Centre with colleagues from the Northern Hokkaido larger parish

Jeep and trailer loaded with tent for Summer Tent Caravan

4

HOKKAIDO CHALLENGES

One of the first Hokkaido challenges we faced was learning to adapt to the Nayoro winters. Nayoro has the reputation of being the coldest city in Japan. Situated in a valley between two ranges of low mountains, winds from Siberia blowing over the western range dumped their snow on our valley. This called for a continual battle with snow during the winter, that usually stretched from November to the end of March. The snow on our street piled up so much that at times children could reach the telephone wires from the banks on the sides of the streets. When we first went to Nayoro there was no regular snow removal system. I had a snow plough made locally, fastened to the front of the Jeep. This had to be raised and lowered manually but with four wheel drive and chains on all four wheels there were not many roads I could not navigate. From the time Dennis was about two he loved to ride in the front seat while I was clearing out our roadway. He would grin from ear to ear as we hit a snow bank and the snow would come billowing over the Jeep in a white cloud. The biggest trouble would come at the spring thaw, when the Jeep would get bogged down in the melting snow and require hours of digging to get released.

Since snow seemed to fall almost every day there was a daily battle to clear the track from the house to the road. There was also the problem of finding a place to put the snow from the sidewalk in front of the house. The best method was using a huge scoop to push the snow and pile it up on the other side of the road. There was also the need to keep our front window clear of the snow falling off the roof. If we didn't remove the snow it would almost be like living in an igloo.

Snow did have its advantages. Nayoro has some of the best skiing in the country. There were two ski hills with ski lifts, only about ten minutes drive from our home. We enjoyed recreation on the ski hills and the children learned to ski almost as soon as they learned to walk. They frequently joined fellow students in all-day school ski excursions. As if to make up for the inclement winters, the spring, summer and fall were gorgeous. In the spring wild cherry trees and purple azaleas would burst into bloom on the mountainsides and dog-toothed violets and trilliums would carpet shady areas under the trees. Summers were warm, but never too hot, and fall was a blaze of colour, reminding us of our Ontario autumns.

In the midst of a busy schedule my one hobby was gardening. This was also something of a challenge. There was a large area to the rear of the house, an open field not cultivated for a number of years where weeds had run rampant. Among these was a kind of twitch grass with a long root system. The battle of the summer was to eradicate this persistent weed without chemicals. The farmer in me couldn't let any of this land go idle, so I set out to cultivate it all. The first summer after we arrived I hit upon an ingenious idea. I would pull a hand plough behind my Jeep. I borrowed the plough from my neighbours, the Kurisu family, and got the son of the family to hold the plough while I drove the Jeep back and forth across the garden. This worked very well except that in order to turn around I encroached somewhat on a neighbour's garden. He complained that the Jeep packed the earth in that section so that he could hardly work it up at all.

The next spring I not only borrowed the Kurisu's plough, but also their horse and had young Mr. Kurisu do the ploughing. A few years later, when hand tractors had been introduced, I hired a man who did custom cultivating to work up the garden with his little tractor.

I tried to grow as wide a variety of vegetables in the garden as possible. I sent to Canada for seeds that were not available locally, like beets, parsnips, broccoli and cauliflower. I also discovered some raspberry and thimble berry plants in Wassamu that had been imported from the United States many years before. I got roots of these and established a large berry patch. I also obtained red currant, black currant and rhubarb roots from missionary friends. Once I got these well established I distributed roots to many Japanese and missionary friends. Much of the garden produce we canned in glass jars. We bought jars fairly cheaply through the Inter-Missionary Services in Tokyo. Each summer we preserved about one hundred jars of fruit and vegetables for the winter season. Neighbours were fascinated by the preserving and soon were ordering jars through us to do their own. After our second home assignment we brought back a large freezer which revolutionized our preservation of fruit and vegetables. This also started a new local craze for frozen foods as freezers became more available in Japan.

EXPANDING OUR HORIZONS
My main energies during the first five years in Nayoro were to help the Rev. Kyoji Tamura carry out his vision of establishing churches or Christian groups in many of the towns and villages of northern Hokkaido. He first scouted through the region to find communities in which there were at least one Christian person. I can remember one historic two-day journey through the north in which we visited Christian contacts in three towns. Five of us crowded into the Jeep for the trip. Besides Mr. Tamura and myself there were Jo Kamatani, the young minister from Wassamu, and two elders from the Nayoro church, Mr. Oikawa and Mr. Sakamoto, who both had cake shops in town. Our first stop was the town of Nakatombetsu, about an hour and a half north-east of Nayoro. The one Christian contact there was the wife of a Junior High School teacher. She welcomed us into her tiny "teacherage" house and agreed to hold monthly meetings in her home for anyone who might want to come.

From Nakatombetsu we proceeded to Esashi, an isolated fishing town on the east coast. There we were greeted by Mr. and Mrs. Murayama, earnest Christians who had formerly held Christian meetings in their home. Mrs. Murayama was a high school teacher and Mr. Murayama was the owner/manager of a large tract of forest. They were eager to have us come for regular meetings in their home. From there we headed inland to the village of Utanobori. Here we met and stayed overnight with the owner of a cake shop who had apprenticed with Mr. Sakamoto in Nayoro. While in Nayoro he had attended the Nayoro church. He also wanted to have house meetings in his home. As a result of this journey we arranged for house meetings to be held on a regular basis in these three communities. Once a month for almost all the time I was in Japan I made a weekend trek to Nakatombetsu and Esashi. I went to Utanobori less frequently. I travelled by train, a two and one half hour trip, starting Saturday afternoon. Saturday evening many high school students and others gathered at the Murayama home for singing, Bible study and fun. I spent the night at the Murayamas. In the afternoon I went to Nakatombetsu. The meeting there soon outgrew the school teacher's home. Mrs. Yuri, the owner of a sewing school offered her large upper sewing room for a children's meeting in the afternoon and for an adult Bible study and discussion meeting in the evening. Forty or fifty children gathered for the children's meetings and eight to ten adults for evening worship and Bible study. After the evening meeting I boarded the train again, arriving back in Nayoro at 1 a.m. I kept up this regular monthly schedule for 25 years. Rev. Hiraga, the minister in Wakkanai, kept the same schedule of house meetings, once a month travelling a similar distance from Wakkanai.

Mrs. Takeda, a widow who had a little store by the sea near the town of Easahi, was one of the people we met through the Esashi house meetings. Rev. Hiraga asked me to go with him to visit Mrs. Takeda who had expressed an interest in learning more about Christianity. Since we both came by train, Mrs. Murayama called a taxi to take us out to Mrs. Takeda's home. When the taxi didn't show up she called again. The office admitted that there wasn't a taxi available at the moment but wondered if a bus would be alright. So the two of us went out in state in a big diesel bus. We found Mrs. Takeda living in a two room house with a little store in front which served the fisher folk who lived in the area. A five year old daughter lived with her. She first became interested in Christianity when she received a letter from her son who was attending university in Tokyo. He had started attending a Seventh Day Adventist church and was thinking of becoming a minister. She decided that she too should find out something about the Christian religion, and since she had heard that Christian meetings were held in Esashi, had started attending the meetings and avidly reading the Bible.

It so happened, that one evening when she was at the meeting in Esashi a thief broke into her store and stole 10,000 yen (about $28.00). It was a tremendous loss for a poor woman like her. To make up the loss she decided to join the fishermen who were fishing for crab at night. The robber was later caught, but without the money. However, far from showing any resentment, she wanted to send him a Bible so that it might teach him a better way of living. She had very quickly grasped some of the essentials of the Christian faith. Her response of love and forgiveness made us wonder if she didn't have a lot to teach us about what it means to be forgiving and supporting Christians.

SUPPORTING NEW MINISTERS

With the help of the Pioneer Evangelism Program, Mr. Tamura and myself gradually came to work with new younger Japanese ministers who took over the work of the new churches. In a few years we had ministers in Shimokawa, Wassamu, Nakagawa, Okoppe and Shibetsu. My role, then, changed from primarily leading house meetings myself to giving support to these new seminary graduates. One of the Kyodan policies for new ministers was that they were not allowed to officiate at the sacraments for two years after they graduated from seminary and had taken an additional examination. This meant that I was called upon to officiate at their churches for baptism and communion services. These usually took place about four times a year. With three or four new ministers to assist at the same time, this in itself kept me busy. In addition, it wasn't long before each of these new ministers had started house meetings in neighbouring towns on their own and asked my help with these from time to time. Sharing services and working with them was a real privilege. At the same time, since all of these minister families had come to Hokkaido from Honshu, to them it was almost like coming to a foreign land. Doreen and I often extended to them our friendship and encouragement for their lonely task.

The first minister to be sent to Okoppe was the Rev. Ishikawa. He and his wife came to Okoppe just a few days after their marriage. They helped to get a church built that included space for a kindergarten. Mr. Ishikawa was the principal of the kindergarten and his wife the head teacher. It wasn't long before Mr. Ishikawa was holding house meetings in the city of Mombetsu, where we had formerly held summer caravans. About once a month I would accompany him to these meetings. He then got the idea that he would like to hold a meeting in the town of Takinoue, which means "above the waterfall." This is a picturesque mountain town but he was not aware of any Christians there.

Mr. Ishikawa made some posters which he put up around the town and a notice in the local newspaper announcing a children's meeting in the afternoon to be followed by an adults' meeting for any who wanted to learn something about Christianity. A few children showed up, but only one adult, Mr. Hamano, a farmer who had come from a mountain farm about twelve kilometres away. He had seen the notice in the paper and had come into town to meet us. With tears in his eyes he said that he had been praying for sixteen years that Christian meetings could be held in his area.

Mr. Hamano had been a day labourer in Osaka living from day to day with little meaning in his life. What little money he earned he spent on liquor. One day he happened to drop into a Christian meeting at which he said he was "converted." He had no formal education and didn't even know how to read. However, the minister told him that a Christian should know how to read the Bible. He started attending primary school, beginning at the third grade and continuing for four years until he could read. After that he moved with his family to a "pioneer farm" in the mountains near Takinoue. He and his sons cleared the trees for his mountainside farm. He finally built himself a new house. He told us, "This house is not mine, it belongs to God, use it in any way you can for God's work." Mr. Ishikawa continued to go to Takinoue once a month and always stayed overnight at the Hamano home. I remember going with him for a Christmas communion service. There were just Mr. and Mrs. Hamano and their two sons, besides Mr. Ishikawa and myself. Sitting on the floor with a candle burning on the low table we joined together in one of the most meaningful sacraments of the Lord's Supper in which I have ever participated. This was not a holy mystery or doctrinal rite reserved for the initiated but a true family love feast symbolizing the love of Jesus for the whole world.

A CHURCH THAT DIED

Sometimes missionaries like to tell about their successes and neglect to mention the failures. I would like to tell the story of the Nakagawa church, a rural church that started out with high hopes but finally ceased to exist. Around 1922 a group of Christian settlers from Honshu decided to form a pioneer farming community near the village of Nakagawa, an isolated community, now one and one half hours by train, but at that time only accessible by the Teshio river. A small church was built, but there was never a resident minister. The story is told of an early Congregational missionary, Mr. Roland, who came from Sapporo once a year, travelled down the river by boat, and spent about a week with the community there. Later, after the building of the railway to Wakkanai, the Japanese minister from Nayoro visited from time to time.

After the war, Dr. Toyohiko Kagawa, hearing of this pioneer rural Christian community, raised enough money to build a church. However, the Hokkaido church authorities decided that a small church so far from any village could never become self supporting. Instead they built a two-storey church in the village of Nakagawa five kilometres from the original community. The lower level of the church was a kindergarten, which could supply some income, and the second storey was the sanctuary. Since the church was so far from the pioneer community and the only transportation was by horse-and-cart or sleigh it meant that most of the Christians in the community only got out to services on special occasions.

The kindergarten was a success, since it was the only kindergarten in the village. The hope had been that the kindergarten could provide some basic Christian education for the young children of the village However, since they were not able to find any Christian kindergarten teachers, the only Christian content was when the Nayoro minister occasionally visited the church.

After I arrived Mr. Tamura and I each had an evening service in Nakagawa once a month. It meant travelling an hour and a half by train for a group of six or eight. Sometimes no one would turn up at all. Because of the train schedule we could not arrive back in Nayoro until 1 o'clock in the morning . For some years there was no direct road by which Nakagawa could be reached. In order to visit in the rural community from time to time it was necessary to walk to the community, visit from house to house and then to spend the night in someone's home. I can remember one night when I stayed in a farm home in the morning I discovered a pile of snow on the floor where it had blown in through the cracks in the sliding doors.

With financial help from the national church for the work in Nakagawa, a summer student, Mr. Miki, was sent to hold regular services and to carry out a more comprehensive visiting program. A year later, after he graduated from theological college, Mr. Miki was sent for a year to live in the community and serve the church there. After he left, a young couple, the Suzukis, were stationed in Nakagawa to serve the church in Nakagawa and to hold more regular services in Nakatombetsu. The Suzukis found this appointment very lonely and left after two years, without a replacement. It was again left to the Nayoro minister and myself to continue the schedule we had before.

The one well-attended Nakagawa service each year was at Christmas. At that time the families from the rural area would make a special effort to attend. In addition the kindergarten children and their parents attended. Fifty or more people crowded into the church. I can remember one Christmas eve

Hokkaido Challenges 65

when Mitsuo Nakamura accompanied me for the Christmas service. We had a lovely Christmas celebration with carols and gifts for all the children. However, during the evening a heavy snow began to fall. By the time we boarded the train it had turned into a raging blizzard. The steam engined train laboured on slowly for some time and finally stopped, stranded in a snow bank. All we could do was to wait until morning when we were rescued by a snow-plow. In the meantime Doreen was home alone with the children. When it got past the usual 1 a.m. return time, she began to worry. Finally, about 6 a.m. she received a phone call from Tomoko Nakamura with the information that the train was stranded and could be expected in some time during the morning. Finally about 11 a.m. I came trudging through the snow from the station. The children saw me coming and called out, "Daddy's coming." At this Doreen broke out in tears of relief. The children called out, "What are you crying for? It's Christmas day."

Through these years there were two faithful elders who had moved into the village of Nakagawa and did what they could to keep the church alive. Finally one of these elders died and only one original member, Mr. Endo, remained. However, some of his actions in the community did not help the church's cause. He got into a fence-line argument with a neighbour and took him to court over about five or six feet of adjoining property. He was very vociferous in standing up for his supposed rights. The Japanese minister from Nayoro tried to mediate but with no success. His action gave the church such a bad name that almost everyone else stopped coming. At about the same time the church building, that had been poorly constructed, began to develop a lean, and the village gave the order that it either be re-built or torn down. The decision was made to turn the kindergarten over to the village to be held in another location. The church building was torn down and the property loaned to the village for a children's playground. After that a few half-hearted efforts were made to hold an occasional house meeting in the home of one family, but finally even this was abandoned.

The question remains: was all that effort over so many years really worthwhile? Sometimes, when I would return home in the small hours of the morning after a fruitless trip, Doreen would say, "Why don't you give up on Nakagawa? They don't appreciate you." However, I do feel that the efforts were not in vain. For the original Christian settlers, the church did what it could in a difficult situation to support them. The older people appreciated that. Even if it was not possible to keep the faith alive in the second and third generations it meant a lot to the pioneers to have someone who cared. In addition, even though they were few in numbers some of the young people and younger families in Nakagawa found meaning in the Christian faith. Some of the young people were baptized but soon moved away in search of work. A few of these made connections with churches in communities to which they moved.

The years that Rev. Miki and the Suzukis were stationed there meant much to the families they came to know. For those years they held regular Sunday School sessions that no doubt left their mark on the children who participated. Even after the ministers had left, Chiyoko Sato, a secretary at the Dohoku Centre, went to Nakagawa once a month for children's meetings. One time when I went with her I observed the enthusiasm of the children and felt that they really appreciated these lively children's meetings.

The fact that the church carried on a kindergarten in a community that would not have otherwise had one showed the parents that the church was concerned about early childhood education that gave the children a better start in their educational training.

In the end it is not for us to judge the success or failure of any Christian endeavour we undertake. We can only believe that if we carry out our service in sincerity and love, those efforts will not be fruitless.

**SHIBETSU CHURCH & THE MINISTRY OF
THE REV. MITSUKO HOSOUMI**
The city of Shibetsu is a city of about 25,000, situated 25 kilometres south of Nayoro. There had been a Presbyterian church

Hokkaido Challenges   67

in Shibetsu from before the war. When the Japanese government forced all the Protestant churches to unite during the war, the Shibetsu Presbyterian church became part of the United Church of Christ in Japan (Kyodan). At the end of the war the Presbyterian churches in Hokkaido decided to withdraw from the Kyodan and continue as the Presbyterian Church in Hokkaido. In Shibetsu, a Presbyterian minister and a small number of Christians carried on the services in the church building there. However, several families who felt a loyalty to the Kyodan withdrew and held regular services in their homes under the leadership of some quite competent lay people. After I arrived to help with the work in the north this group asked if Mr. Tamura and I would meet with them from time to time. Before long they asked the Hokkaido District of the Kyodan if they could be included in the Pioneer Evangelism Plan. While the Rev. Kamatani was serving in Wassamu, he provided leadership for the work in Shibetsu as well. After the Kamatanis left Wassamu it was decided that the two churches would become a two point pastoral charge to be served from Shibetsu, since it was the larger community. Shibetsu church was included in the Pioneer Evangelism Plan with financial assistance for the church building and partial support for a minister.

The Rev. Mistuko Hosoumi was appointed to head up this work. Mitsuko was the first woman minister to serve in the northern region. She came from Tokyo where she had been working for several years as an assistant in a Kyodan church. Mitsuko had a rather arduous life. She had grown up in Tokyo during the war and had faced many hardships as a result of the bombing and lack of good nutrition. She contracted tuberculosis and spent several years in a sanitarium. While in the sanitarium she had her first contact with Christianity. It changed her life's direction. On leaving the hospital she attended the Japan Biblical Seminary to become a minister. This Seminary is a night school which enabled students to work their way through seminary along with a daytime job. In this way Mitsuko was ordained as a minister at a time when women ministers were few in number. After several years in the inner city church, she decided she would rather work on her own and volunteered to serve in a rural church in Hokkaido. At first we wondered how a "city girl" would fit into a mostly rural church. We were pleasantly surprised. She related particularly well to the farm families that made up a significant part of the Christians in Wassamu and Shibetsu. She lived in an upper room over the kindergarten and served as both the minister of the church and the principal of the kindergarten. Before long they had a kindergarten of about 40 children with two teachers. On Sunday, church services were held in the Shibetsu church in the morning and the Wassamu church in the afternoon.

Since Mitsuko did not have a car I accompanied her to house meetings in rural communities and visitation to farm homes. Once a month I would accompany her to the house church in Kenbuchi in the home of postal worker, Noriyoshi Ishizaki. We also went once a month to the village of Asahi where a doctor and his wife had their joint medical practice. Since the wife was a Christian she opened her home for house meetings and invited others from the community to attend. There was a particularly good response from the young people, who were attracted by the singing of hymns around the doctor's electric organ.

The effectiveness of Miss Hosoumi's work with young people is illustrated by a story I recorded in my 1969 yearly report. This is the account of a third year high school girl named Ito who lived on a farm in the country some distance from Wassamu. She had heard about Christianity through a Bible-study radio broadcast and started attending the Wassamu church. Shortly before Christmas she wrote to Miss Hosoumi asking to be baptized. She arranged for Miss Ito to be baptized along with seven other people in January. I assisted in this baptism. I learned then that Miss Ito had made her decision in spite of opposition from her grandparents and discouragement from her parents. Miss Ito promised to help with the Sunday School in the Wassamu church. During her ministry in Shibetsu and Wassamu many young people were baptized, but because most of them moved away to attend college or go to work the

Hokkaido Challenges 69

continuing membership never seemed to increase. This never seemed to discourage Miss Hosoumi, who said, "Our task as a church is to send people out as Christians into the world."

Miss Hosoumi served Shibetsu and Wassamu for the rest of her ministry. She had a continual battle with diabetes and had to retire to a Christian senior's residence near Sapporo. I visited her there for the last time on one of my trips back to Japan. She was overjoyed to sit with me on a bench beside a stream flowing by the residence and recalling the many happy and fruitful times we had in our ministry together. I received word several years later that she had died. The Shibetsu and Wassamu churches sent many tributes for the faithfulness of her service with them.

Rev. Tamura with Floyd drinking tea

5

COMMUNITY ENGAGEMENT

One of the dreams that Alf Stone had for our work in Nayoro was the establishment of a northern Japan "rural community centre." It was not long before Mr. Tamura and I shared the dream. There had been several rural community centres established in Honshu. Two of these had included small "model farms" along with leadership training facilities both for training lay church leaders and for providing practical assistance to farming communities facing major government farm-policy changes in post-war Japan. Mr. Tamura and I got information about these centres and started some planning of our own. We explored the possibilities of a small farm with accommodation for the training of church leaders and for rural youth.

We scouted the area for cheap hillside land that might be developed into such a centre. We soon came to realize that such land might not be practical since hillside land would almost be inaccessible in winter when much of our training would need to be carried on. We then began to look at land closer to Nayoro. We found a plot of about 20 acres not far from the city. We drew up a plan with estimates for buying the land, putting up a training centre, buying a small tractor and implements and developing a farm operation. This was presented to the Hokkaido District Executive of the United Church of Christ in Japan. However, they persuaded us that a small operation of this sort would never become a "model" and that the cost would be prohibitive. I also realized that, although I had grown up on a farm, I was not an agricultural expert and that most of my energy would have to be put into keeping the farm functioning with little time left over for training and outreach. I felt that they had given us very sound advice.

Having discarded the idea of a farm we concentrated on finding a suitable place for a community type centre that could serve as a training facility for the lay church leaders of the northern region, a centre for the training of rural youth in better methods of farming and a Community Centre that would be available to the people of the region for a wide variety of purposes. We were fortunate in finding a suitable location at the edge of the city, ten minutes walk from the station and near the Agricultural High School. The plot of land had been the site of an abandoned brick factory. We persuaded the eighty year old owner to sell us the land for a reasonable price and immediately began drawing up plans for the centre building. The plans were approved by the Executive of the Hokkaido District of the United Church of Christ and a grant from the United Church of Canada was requested. The total cost of the land, building and equipment came to about $14,000. This low price was possible because at the time the exchange rate was 360 yen to the Canadian dollar.

The main building was a two storey cement block construction with a wing of stucco that included bath, toilets and living quarters for a Japanese director. The building provided sleeping quarters for 40 people, eating accommodations for 60 and seating room for about 80. Much credit for the low cost of construction was given to Rev. Kyoji Tamura who had extensive experience with building and was able to negotiate a good contract. Considerable volunteer labour was also provided by church and high school youth groups.

The Northern Hokkaido Christian Centre or the "Dohoku Centre" as it came to be called, was dedicated on September 19th, 1960 with church leaders, the Mayor of Nayoro, Mr. Kotaro Ikeda, and many community people attending. The title "dohoku" was the Japanese word used to refer to the northern region of Hokkaido. The northern region served an area that stretched from Asahigawa, a city of some 350,000 with three Kyodan churches, through to Wakkanai at the northern tip of the island.

The mayor suggested that if we wanted the centre to be used by the whole community, it would be better to refer to it simply as the "Dohoku Centre," rather than "Dohoku Christian Centre." He rightly reasoned that some people might come more readily to a facility not specifically labelled as Christian.

Among activities carried out in the Dohoku Centre that fall were local church young peoples' rallies, three "open house" events for students of local high schools, a 4-H Club Youth gathering, a Hokkaido Rural Church Youth event and a school teachers' winter retreat.

The first January we experimented with a program centred on Bible study. About fifteen people participated. Contrary to our expectations a large proportion of those who attended were non-Christians wanting to learn more about the Bible. In Japan the Christian Bible is readily available in book stores and annually on a "best sellers" list. One young student, who had never studied the Bible, decided that on her return home she would read two chapters of the Bible a day and save up questions to ask me when I visited her town once a month. She and a friend started a Bible study group for fellow high school students.

We also developed a Japanese church tradition of holding two day "shuyokai" training session retreats. These included worship, often led by lay people, along with Bible study in small groups. These events were planned to include both younger and older people related to all the Kyodan churches and house meetings in northern Hokkaido. Planning for these was carried out not just by Centre staff but in cooperation with lay and clergy leaders of the regional churches.

SUMMER ENGLISH CAMPS

A popular program, begun in 1961, and which carried on successfully for many years, was summer English conversation camps for Junior High and Senior High students. For these the facilities were always filled to capacity. Sometimes we had to put up tents for extra accommodation. We recruited English speaking teachers from many parts of Japan to join us for a week of their summer vacation. The "English Camps" ran for about four days each. Daytime was taken up with a schedule of English conversation, pronunciation and sentence drill in groups of six or eight with an English speaking teacher and a Japanese teacher's assistant. The evenings, however, were given over to discussion in Japanese on topics of the students' own choice. This was an opportunity they relished, since dis-

cussion was discouraged in their schools. Topics chosen ranged from "competition for college entrance" and "boy-girl relationships" to "our purpose in life" and the "existence of God."
The English Camps proved to be an excellent opportunity of getting in touch with students. No attempt was made to use these as a means of Christian proselytism, but only to respond to the felt needs of the students themselves. Some students were influenced by the ethos of the camps themselves and did go on to explore what Christianity had to offer, but this was never a major thrust of the camps. Many students appreciated the opportunity to discuss issues that were important to them. They began to question the nature of both the educational and the political system of the country and many went on to become social activists working for social change. We sometimes considered our activities as a kind of fifth column outside the regular Japanese educational system. A number of the teachers we recruited as assistants went back to their schools attempting to introduce some measure of discussion and to raise social consciousness among their students.

MITSUO NAKAMURA
The first director, and my co-worker in establishing the programmes of the Dohoku Centre, was Mitsuo Nakamura. Mitsuo came with valuable experience in agriculture. He also had attended the Tokyo Theological Seminary and served as a student assistant in Dr. Toyohiko Kagawa's Tokyo church.
Mitsuo grew up on an Hokkaido farm and attended the high school division of the Nopporo Agricultural College. At this Christian-based institution he had his first contact with Christianity through student Bible study groups and chapel services. On graduation he felt called to the Christian ministry and entered the Tokyo Theological Seminary. His father was very much opposed to his decision and disowned him for his action. He was not allowed to return home during his time in the Seminary. Fortunately, his mother kept in contact and sent him food from the farm from time to time. On graduation he returned to the Agricultural College as student chaplain. When we were looking for a director for the Dohoku Centre, I

approached Dr. Makoto Hiura, the President of the College. He highly recommended Mitsuo and proposed that the Dohoku Centre be a northern outpost for the Three Love School Programme that they had established in the College. We held our first Three Love School in January of 1961. It later became a central part of our programming. Mitsuo gave outstanding leadership in the Three Love Programme over the years. His wife, Tomoko, was a Home Economics High School and gave valuable assistance with planning Centre meals for our various programmes. She also provided leadership in training farm young people in food and nutrition issues.

Many of the innovative programmes we developed in the Dohoku Centre owed a great deal to Mitsuo's insights and initiative. He helped to establish the Dohoku Centre English Conversation School and became its Business Manager. With the income from the school we hired an Assistant Director of the Dohoku Centre in 1971. Dr. Hiura recommended Hyoe Watanabe, another graduate of the Agricultural College. Hyoe and his wife Shizue also made valuable contributions to the life of the Centre of which I will speak later.

Mitsuo Nakamura had always been concerned about the political life of the community and nation. After he had served on the staff of the Centre for fifteen years he was approached by the local Socialist Party Executive to be their candidate for Mayor of Nayoro. After much soul searching he decided to accept their nomination. The election campaign proceeded very well. The candidate for the Liberal Democratic Party was a newcomer to politics, not well known in the community. There was also a third party candidate who threatened to split the Liberal Democratic vote. When it appeared that Mitsuo was almost certain to win, the Liberal Democratic Party became alarmed. They replaced their candidate with an older man who had many people in the city under obligation to him. The "third party candidate" was persuaded to back out and although Mitsuo made a good showing, he was not able to win the Mayoralty position. However, at the next election he won a Council seat and served with distinction for about eight years. For several years after being elected to Council he continued as Manager of the English School and Hyoe Watanabe took over as Centre Director. After completing several terms on the Council, Mitsuo decided not to run again and accepted the post as minister of the Wakkanai church, much to the satisfaction of his wife, Tomoko, who preferred him doing the work of a minister to that of a politician.

ORIGINS OF THE THREE LOVE MOVEMENT: DR. TOYOHIKU KAGAWA

One of the most important programmes of the Dohoku Centre and the one that is most representative of our attempt to move beyond churchianity to a community and world centred Christianity was the three love movement. To get back to the earliest example of this movement we need to go to the life and work of Dr. Toyohiko Kagawa.

As a youth I had heard the story of Kagawa. He was born in Kobe in 1888, the son of a second "concubine wife" of his wealthy father. Both his father and his mother died when he was very young, and he was sent to be adopted by his father's legal wife who resented him and showed him no love. He did well in school and on reaching high school age went to live with a rich uncle. Wanting to learn English, he visited the home of a Presbyterian missionary, Dr. Harry Myers. This became a major turning point in his life. He began to study the Bible devotedly. He was baptized and decided to go to a seminary. His uncle objected, disowned him and sent him out of the house. However, Dr. Myers got him a scholarship that enabled him to go a theological seminary in Kobe. Out of his love for God and humanity Kagawa began to preach in the slums of Kobe. Through this experience he realized that he could never really communicate with people in the slums unless he lived among them. On Christmas Eve of 1909 he moved into a room in Shinkawa, a famous slum district of Kobe. He had not been there long when a beggar showed up at the door. On finding that Kagawa was living all alone, he said, "This is much too big for one person, I'll come and live with you." At first his inclination was to refuse, but then he thought, "I have come to demonstrate to the people here the love of Christ, how can I say 'No'?" The beggar moved in with him and before long two others joined him sharing their life and meals together.

While still living in the slums Kagawa also preached at a little chapel. One young woman who came to hear him preach was Haruko Shiba. She was later baptized and helped in the work of the chapel. When her family tried to marry her off to a non-Christian, and when Kagawa discovered that she too was prepared to live and work in the slums, they were married and continued a faithful ministry together for their whole lifetimes.

In 1915 Kagawa went to the United States to study at Princeton University. While he was away Haruko went to a Bible training school in Yokohama. When he came back they went back to work together in the Shinakawa slums of Kobe. In 1923, after the great earthquake in Yokohama and Tokyo, they moved to Tokyo to aid the homeless and destitute there. This became the centre of a new mission of social service, writing, and Christian outreach to the whole nation. In 1930 he helped to found the Kingdom of God Movement in an effort to evangelize every group and class in the nation working with farmers, industrial workers, fishing-folk, miners, transport workers and public service workers. He organized the first of the labour unions in Japan and spent some time in jail for his organizing efforts. His concern for the struggling and poverty stricken farmers caused him to organize a "National Peasants' Union" and to help develop credit unions and rural cooperatives. This was the beginning of the rural cooperative movement that eventually involved most of the farmers in Japan and still exists today.

He was not averse to entering into the political fray. After studying the political movements of several countries he helped to organize the first Labour Party of Japan. In all his work within the social movements he did not hide the fact that he was a Christian but he never sought to foist his Christianity on anyone. In his book, Love the Law of Life, he says, "I served as a Good Samaritan, but they knew that I was a Christian. Many of my friends found the nature of Christianity through this service."

I learned from Kagawa that it was sufficient to do the work of a Good Samaritan in the spirit of Jesus, and not try to get others to accept my beliefs.

THREE LOVE MOVEMENT IN HOKKAIDO

The Three Love Movement in Hokkaido began in 1950 under the leadership of Dr. Makoto Hiura, the Principal of the Nopporo Agricultural College, a Christian-based two year junior college for rural Hokkaido youth. The Three Love Schools, although relying on much the same spirit as the rural gospel schools, involved a major shift in emphasis and programme. First, the name change to "Three Love Schools" was significant. The "three loves," love for God, love for people and love for the earth, was based on a concept coming out of the Danish "folk school" movement in which some of the Agricultural College staff had participated.

Three Love Schools were conceived as a holistic approach, including the spiritual, the social and a concern for the land and the agricultural way of life. The target group was not those already in the college system, but other rural youth who could not afford to attend college but wanted practical training. Using the Nopporo Agricultural College facilities, the Three Love Schools were held during the spring two-week vacation period at very little cost to the participants who were encouraged to bring their own food and even their "futon" bedding. The main courses offered were on better agricultural methods and on personal and community ways of living.

DOHOKU CENTRE THREE LOVE SCHOOLS

Since most of those who attended the Three Love Schools in Nopporo were from the central region of Hokkaido it was felt that shorter schools in the northern region would fulfill a real need. The Dohoku Centre Three Love Schools were started in January of 1961. We developed a pattern of four-day schools in January and two-day schools in August. Planning for all these schools was held in conjunction with past participants, looking at the current needs of rural youth and building programmes to meet their needs. Once the issues had been identified, we began looking for leaders to bring input. We were fortunate in being able to draw on teachers from the agricultural college, but we also found many leaders from the surrounding community.

Over the years the Three Love Schools dealt with a wide variety of topics. In addition to various aspects of scientific agriculture there were studies on home and community living, male-female relationships, critique of government agricultural policies and rural cooperatives. In March of 1966 after one of our Three Love Schools I wrote in a letter to friends in Canada:

> Throughout the school it was more and more recognized that better farming methods alone would not solve rural problems. Farmers must learn to work together and must learn to take more effective political action on government policies harmful to farmers. There was considerable interest in various methods of cooperative farming as a means of overcoming the inefficiency of small scale operations. The director of a nearby fifteen family Cooperative Dairy Farm with a herd of 200 cows told of some of their hopes for more support for the dairy industry and their difficulties in working effectively as a cooperative with so many families involved.

One of the study sessions I remember in particular was with some leaders of a hot-house vegetable growing cooperative in the Lake Doya region. One summer the active volcano at Lake Doya had erupted spewing ash over much of the surrounding territory. By working together in the Cooperative the group was able to help those most badly affected to restore their land and their green-houses in order to continue their agricultural production.

The Three Love Schools tried to keep abreast of the times by dealing with practical issues as they arose. In my 1976 newsletter I remarked that one of the sectors of Japanese society hurting most is the rural population:

Caught in the cost-price squeeze of rising costs for farm input and falling prices for their produce many farmers are heavily in debt. This year in Hokkaido because of bad weather, there was a poor rice crop, and it is likely that many more farmers will go bankrupt and have to move off the land. Farmers in Japan, like many in Canada, suffer from government policies which favour the big corporations and discriminate against farmers. The church needs to be sharing their pain and joining with the farmers in their struggle for a better and fuller life.

During the Three Love Schools pre-breakfast, Bible study sessions related Bible passages to some of the rural issues being discussed. Although 95 per cent of those who attended Three Love Schools were non-Christian, many of them found help in the truths for life from the Bible. There was no pressure to become Christians, but rather participants were encouraged to include some of the principles they found in the Bible in daily living. A few did eventually become Christian but the majority continued with their family religion, usually Buddhism or Shintoism, with new dimensions.

One girl said that before she came she was a little worried because this was a Christian sponsored school, but after taking part she realized that there was something more she needed in finding a faith to live by. Another woman who had attended four Three Love Schools said that she couldn't stay away since the schools gave her the strength she needs to tackle the often discouraging tasks at home. She had been attending church for several years, even though it meant walking six kilometres to catch a train to the church in Okoppe and then returning the same way at night after the service was over.

Many of these young people would never become Christians, but old prejudices against Christianity were broken down and the way opened for dialogue between the church and rural society. To me this is the central meaning of the mission of the church in the world - to listen, to learn, to serve practical needs of people and to share with them in their struggles.

THE MINAMATA CONNECTION

Minamata is a fishing town in the southern island of Kyushu which became infamous throughout Japan and the world for the emergence of the "Minamata disease." For several years many of the citizens of Minamata were crippled and dying from a mysterious plague which especially hit the fisher-folk of the area. Finally the source was traced to a fertilizer plant which was discharging raw mercury-laden effluent into the harbour. The fish had been poisoned, and since the families of the fishermen ate large quantities of the fish they formed the largest group of victims. When this became known the citizens began a campaign to stop the discharge and to get compensation for the hundreds of families that had been affected. In a video made of the fishermen's action I vividly remember a scene of a woman from Minamata sitting on the table immediately in front of the corporation head manager in Tokyo, demanding an end to the pollution and compensation for the victims. Their efforts finally paid off, the pollution was stopped and affected families were given financial help to start new businesses.

Because the whole harbour and the sea in the surrounding area were permanently polluted it was no longer possible for the fisher-folk to make a living. Instead they abandoned fishing and started to plant orange orchards on the hillsides surrounding the town. However, because of their experience with mercury poisoning, they vowed to grow their oranges organically.

The Dohoku Centre Three Love Schools, which had been studying organic agriculture, invited several members of the Minamata organic orange growers cooperative to come to Nayoro to tell their story. We were all greatly impressed by their dramatic account, but we also heard of some of the difficulties they were facing. Because they did not use pesticides or artificial colouring, their oranges sometimes had blemishes. This meant that the large retailers refused to sell their produce and they had to find other markets. Participants in the Three Love Schools set out to become their marketing agents in many parts of Hokkaido. For instance, every year in December and again in February the Dohoku Centre arranged to have a large truckload of oranges shipped to Nayoro for distribution in the area. Three Love School members from other parts of Hokkaido also made similar arrangements.

DR. MAKOTO HIURA

When we began the Dohoku Three Love Schools Dr. Hiura became our most important supporter and mentor. He made a point of being present and giving leadership at almost all the Three Love Schools.

One of the anticipated features of every Three Love School was a talk by Dr. Hiura on the Three Love Spirit. He shared some of the origins of the "three love idea" in the folk schools of Denmark. He told about his own search as a young man for meaning in life. In his teens he had his first contact with Christianity when he happened to drop into a church building and was attracted by the message he heard there. Later, when he went to Sapporo to attend the Hokkaido University, he began to attend the Sapporo Congregational Church. He mentioned that he was attracted by the fact that in the church although there were "lectures," something like a university, there were no tuition fees and everyone was welcome. This gave him the idea for a university without fees, one of the bases for the Three Love Schools within the Nopporo Agricultural College. Within a year he said he had decided to become a Christian and was baptized.

Most of the farm youth who attended our Three Love Schools knew very little about Christianity. Dr. Hiura made no attempt to force the Christian faith on them, but did speak of the value of the Bible in finding a meaning to life and guidance in building a new rural society based on cooperation rather than competition. He spoke of the need to find a faith in a spirit beyond their own if they were to become leaders dedicated to their communities. He spoke of "love for God," not in any narrow doctrinal way but as the power of love outside ourselves, the source of our being. When he spoke of the Bible it was related to the real life issues and situations we were discussing in the seminars and lectures. He spoke of love as the source of life and mutual love among people as the basis for a successful rural society. To farm youth who might be attracted by the bright lights and prosperity of the city he recommended getting rooted in the soil and of maintaining and reforming rural communities.

The Three Love School at the Dohoku Centre was the first of many regional schools developed throughout Hokkaido in places like Kitami, Setana, Kami-Furano, Nakashibetsu and in the Tokachi area.

In 1964 after a dispute with the Board of Governors Dr. Hiura was forced to resign as President of the Agricultural College, perhaps because he was putting so much effort into the "free" Three Love Schools. However, he was so well respected by the students of the College that they supported him strongly and held a strike for several weeks to try to get him reinstated, but to no avail. Even after his retirement as President in 1964 he stayed on at the College as President Emeritus, continuing to do research and participating in Three Love Schools throughout Hokkaido. After his resignation as President, the Three Love Schools at the College were discontinued. From that point the Dohoku Centre became the co-ordinating body for the other Three Love Schools throughout Hokkaido. This responsibility fell primarily to Mitsuo Nakamura and later to Hyoe Watanabe, Directors of the Dohoku Centre.

Dr. Hiura was perhaps one of the most important influences in my thinking with regard to mission in Japan and my relation to rural people. After his death in 1990 I was asked to contribute to a book of memorial tributes to Dr. Hiura. In my message I told how he helped me relate the Christian faith to the rural people of Japan. His message was: It is difficult for rural people to become Christians quickly. For rural people to become Christian it is probably necessary to wait till the next generation.

It was this advice more than anything else that persuaded me to stay in Nayoro throughout the whole of my career in Japan. The following story bears out the truth of his advice. I saw for myself how prophetic his words had been. Towards the end of my stay in Japan I was asked by the minister of the Shibetsu church, Rev. Mitsuko Hosoumi, to go with her to visit a farm home in the country. She had learned that someone in this home had subscribed to a Bible study course provided by an inter-church radio broadcast. We found a Junior High School girl taking the course at her father's recommendation. He had attended one of the first Three Love Schools at the Agricultural College. He had been much attracted to the study of the Bible, but since he was the eldest son taking over the family farm it was impossible for him to break away from his family traditions. However, when he became head of the household, he greatly desired that his children be influenced by the teachings of the Bible. His daughter began to attend church in Shibetsu. She was baptized, took kindergarten teacher's training and became a teacher in the Nopporo church kindergarten.

Dr. Makoto Hiura was not only the founder of the Three Love movement that became the centre-piece of my work in Japan, he was also my inspiration, my mentor and beloved friend. I give thanks for getting to know such an extremely practical and deeply spiritual man.

THREE LOVE SCHOOL PARTICIPANTS WHO MADE A DIFFERENCE

If I searched them out I could probably find stories of hundreds of participants of fifty years of Three Love Schools at the Nopporo Agricultural College, the Dohoku Centre and other regional schools who have made a big difference in their homes, their own communities and in national life of Japan. I mention here just a few.

THE IGARASHI FAMILY OF CHIEBUN

One of the young men to attend our first Three Love School in 1961 was Masaru Igarashi, who grew up on a vegetable farm in Chiebun, a rural community just north of Nayoro. He graduated from the Nopporo Agricultural College and had a great respect for Dr. Hiura. We recruited him to help plan our early Three Love Schools. His wife, Itsuko, helped to organize programs for women, especially for the summer two day "homemaking parties" as they were called. Masaru's younger sister, Miyo, also took part in the Three Love Schools and later became

Office Secretary for our Dohoku English Conversation School. Masuru took an active part in local politics and was elected for one term as the representative on the Hokkaido Prefecture Assembly. Later he became President of the local Farmers' Cooperative. The Igarashi family gave solid support to the work of the Three Love program.

KIMIKO AND YOSHIMARO HOMMA

One of many "three love marriages" of couples who became acquainted at Three Love Schools was that of Kimiko Matsuda and Yoshimaro Homma. I first came to know Kimiko when she was in high school in Esashi, a fishing village on the northeast coast of Hokkaido. She attended the house meeting in the home of the Murayamas to which I went once a month. Kimiko attended these meetings faithfully and on graduation from high school was looking for a job. We needed a secretary for the Centre and I invited her to come to Nayoro with her widowed mother. She was an amiable and effective secretary and also assisted in planning Three Love Schools and serving meals. Yoshimaro came to several Three Love Schools and they fell in love and were married.

Yoshimaro worked on his father's dairy farm near the city of Mombetsu. Kimiko had a difficult time at first since her mother-in-law was opposed to Kimiko's Christian faith. Yoshimaro was supportive but it was difficult for Kimiko to attend church regularly. Two boys were born into the family and her life became busier than ever. At least once a year she would arrange to get back to Nayoro for a visit and a chance to attend church. Yoshimaro gradually took over the farm and after the mother died, life became somewhat easier for Kimiko. Yoshimaro developed the dairy herd, became a leader in the community and the head of the local farmers' co-op. Both of them now make important contributions in the leadership of the rural community life.

MICHIKO KUBO AND TOSHIMITSU MIYAJIMA

The Kubo family had a small vegetable farm at the edge of the city of Nayoro. We got to know the Kubo family through buying vegetable seedlings from them each spring. Michiko began attending the Nayoro church and became a leader in the young people's group. With a farm background she eagerly participated in the first Three Love Schools where she met Toshimitsu Miyajima.

Toshimitsu Miyajima grew up on a farm near the mountain-ringed village of Onnebetsu, about 40 kilometres from Nayoro. He was a graduate of the High School Department of the Nopporo Agricultural College. He came to our first three Three Love Schools. He was not a Christian but was attracted by the program which promised practical training in agriculture and rural youth leadership. He responded positively to the morning Bible study sessions with Dr. Hiura. Friendship blossomed between Toshimitsu and Michiko and they were married. However, one month after their wedding Toshimitsu went to California on an agricultural training project. Michiko lived with her mother-in-law for a time and later came to assist us at the Dohoku Centre in the office. In California Toshimitsu began to attend a Japanese church where he was baptized. On coming back to Japan he and Michiko came to our house to talk over the possibility of attending a theological college in preparation for rural Christian service. We suggested that they go to the Rural Theological Seminary in Tsurukawa, south of Tokyo. Michiko took kindergarten teacher's training and then got a teaching job to help pay his way through seminary. After three years of theological training for Toshimitsu, and ministry in Wakayama in 1980, they were sent to a three point pastoral charge on the Hidaka peninsula in southern Hokkaido known for its large concentration of Ainu, the aboriginal people of Hokkaido.

As Toshimitsu and Michiko ministered to the Ainu people, many of whom lived in poverty, he learned the history of discrimination and outright persecution to which they had been subjected. He became aware of the struggle of the Ainu people against the invading Japanese colonists from the early 1500's, the Japanese gradually forcing the Ainu into villages in the less desirable areas of the island. Since there was no comprehensive Japanese history of this struggle, Toshimitsu decided to write a book that has been translated into English by my successor,

Rob Witmer, and published by the United Church of Canada Publishing House. *The Land of Elms - The History, Culture and Present Day Situation of the Ainu People* is a fascinating, well-written and most definitive book yet written on the history of the Ainu people. Toshimitsu's motivation in writing this book shows an aspect of Christian mission which is fundamental to the gospel, that of responding to discrimination and injustice wherever it is found and working for the rights and freedoms of all people. I am convinced that one of the places in which Toshimitsu Miyajima gained this vision was in the Three Love School programmes.

THE DOHOKU CENTRE ENGLISH SCHOOL

For some time after its founding, the Dohoku Centre considered how it might become more financially self supporting while at the same time providing a needed service to the community. The opportunity to do this came in the spring of 1970 when we bought the rights to an English night school which had been operated successfully by Mr. Yamamoto, a Japanese teacher of English who had decided to move to Tokyo.

Doreen and I were part-time teachers. Japanese teachers helped students with their school English text lessons while we concentrated on conversational English and pronunciation. We had a total of 350 students in Nayoro and in branch schools in Shimokawa and Shibetsu. We were joined on staff in the fall of 1970 by Gordon Morwood, son of Phyllis Morwood, a relative of Doreen. Gordon came to us after graduation from McMaster University and stayed for two years. He became like another son living with us as a member of the family.

Gordon was an enthusiastic teacher in the English school and in the other activities of the Dohoku Centre. In a 1971 Christmas letter, written to friends in Canada toward the end of his stay, Gord shared some important insights into the work both of the English school and the Dohoku Centre:

> The work done by the Dohoku Centre has shown me what real Christianity is. The programmes are constructed to make the Centre a place of real encoun-

ter for those who participate - encounter with new people and new ideas, and in working through those problems which inevitably appear, they often come up with new discoveries about themselves and others around them. This is the main thrust of the English camps, and some real leaders are beginning to appear, just as leaders have appeared from the ranks of the young farm people, and the working young people of Nayoro, with whom the centre has done much work.

During the summer of 1971, Gord's girlfriend, Jane Lowe, came to visit him. In the same letter, Gord describes this visit as the most important event of his life:

> It was a tremendous experience being able to introduce Jane to my friends and share some of my life with her. This shared experience provided the levels of understanding between us which developed into the most important commitment of our lives - we are engaged to be married next August.

There is an interesting story about how this engagement took place. At the time they came to their commitment, Gord was sick in bed with a serious throat infection. He was too sick to go out to buy an engagement ring so he commissioned our daughter Susan, who was home for summer vacation, to go to town with Jane to pick out the ring. That engagement led to a very happy and fruitful marriage.

The influence of the Dohoku Centre on Gordon's life helped him to define his focus. After graduation in social work at the University of Calgary, he served for several years in Alberta coordinating services for the handicapped in rural areas. During his subsequent career he served as Director of Social Planning in Niagara Falls, National Program Director of the Canadian Mental Health Association, the Director of St. Christopher House in Toronto and for the Family Services Appeal organization for the Peel District. His work with the Dohoku Centre and English School helped set his sights on a social service career through which he has made remarkable contributions to Canadian society.

ALAN McLEAN

After Gord returned to Canada we were happy to welcome Alan McLean as the new English teacher from the fall of 1972 to 1975. Alan also lived with us and became part of the family, making many close friends and becoming quite proficient in Japanese. His parents came to visit him in the summer of 1973 and he took them on a tour of Japan. Alan was a voracious reader and devoured the books in my library. He became particularly interested in "liberation theology" and on his return to Canada entered Emmanuel College graduating with a postgraduate scholarship. He also spent a year working with the World Christian Student Federation in Geneva. He has served as a United Church minister in churches in Woodville, Markham and Hamilton.

DAVID THOMPSON

In our Christmas letter in 1973 we happened to mention that we were looking for another teacher to take Alan's place in the summer of 1975. This brought a response from an old friend, David Thompson, who we had come to know when he had been stationed in Wakkanai with the U.S. Air Force. The chaplain at the U.S. base had several times brought servicemen to the Dohoku Centre for weekend retreats. David was among one of these groups. Up until that time he had been bored with life at the base and as an African American was afraid to step off the base into the Japanese community, not knowing what kind of reception he would have. However, after a weekend at the Centre his whole attitude changed. We introduced him to Japanese friends at the Wakkanai church where he began teaching English. He said afterwards, "I just began living then!"

After leaving Japan he was stationed for a time in Frankfurt, Germany, where we arranged to meet him on our return to Canada by way of Europe in 1968. In his letter to us in 1975 he told us that he had left the Air Force, taken teacher's training in New York, was ready to teach, and said, "How about me for your school?" David came to Nayoro and spent some of the happiest years of his life teaching English and became very popular with both students and parents. Before he left he even preached a sermon in Japanese. His appointment was also most unusual. He was a Baptist, sent out by the U.S. Methodist Church to serve with the United Church of Canada. After returning to the United States he taught for several years in inner-city Los Angeles, but finding this too stressful, has taken up office work in the business world.

JAPANESE TEACHERS OF ENGLISH

The English School was fortunate in the calibre of the Japanese staff it had through the years. In particular two of the first teachers, Yoko Ueda and Chieko Mizushima, helped to establish the pattern for the school and get it on a firm footing. Yoko Ueda subsequently went to Canada where she attended York University, earned a doctorate, and is now working with a university in the United States coordinating recruitment of students from Japan. Chieko Mizushima married a Japanese school teacher in eastern Hokkaido. The whole staff was invited to the wedding. The Japanese teachers of English gave extra coaching to school-age students and assisted the overseas teachers with conversational English classes. Once a week for half of a fifty minute period, the overseas teachers taught conversation and pronunciation to each class. After the school had been well established, we gave the teachers an opportunity for a one month overseas experience in Canada or the United States. This helped improve their skills and represented an extra bonus for their dedication.

As overseas financial support for the Dohoku Centre was gradually reduced and finally eliminated, the income from the English school did much to keep the Centre solvent. At the same time it fulfilled a real need in the community for English conversation training. Many of its graduates went on to become quite fluent in English and took places of leadership in the communities in which they lived and worked.

KOINONIA YOUTH GROUP

In the spring of 1965 the Dohoku Centre, in cooperation with the Nayoro Church, launched a community based youth group for working young people in the town. It was patterned after a similar group started two years previously in Asahigawa by missionary Rudolf Kuyten and the Asahigawa churches. They had chosen the Greek word "koinonia" with its meaning of "love" and "community" as the name for their group. The Nayoro Koinonia met twice a month for discussion on topics of concern to young people and for community service projects. For instance they took responsibility for planting and maintaining flower beds in the boulevard of the main street.

They sponsored a public meeting featuring Dr. Iwamura, Japan's first overseas doctor to Nepal. Dr. Iwamura told a fascinating story of bringing medical service to a country with few medical facilities and of their own adoption of Nepalese children. Another service project of the Koinonia group was working with mentally handicapped children and their mothers and raising money for a Centre for handicapped children in Nayoro.

The Koinonia group provided an opportunity for church related youth and non-church youth to work together on projects for the whole community. It became an important place for dialogue and community outreach. We even had our first "koinonia" wedding for a couple, who although not themselves Christians wanted a "Christian style" wedding. Mitsuo Nakamura officiated at a beautiful wedding on the grounds of the Centre.

NORTHERN REGION COMMUNITY OUTREACH

One of the goals of the Dohoku Centre was to participate in community outreach along with the churches of the northern region. One of the ways in which it attempted to do this was by holding "film nights" in isolated rural communities. One of these communities was a pioneer farming settlement in the hills not far from the city of Nayoro. After the war the Japanese government had opened up new land for repatriated farmers from the Sakhalin Island to the north of Hokkaido that had been taken over by Russia after the Japanese defeat. The government took responsibility for clearing the land, giving assistance for the building of houses and the building of a school. Each farm family was given from 25 to 50 acres of land. With this they were expected to raise crops and eventually become financially independent.

We decided to have a film night in the school house in the winter for the whole community. However, because the area was completely inaccessible by car during the winter, we borrowed our neighbour Mr. Kurisu's horse and sleigh for the journey. Wally Brownlee, our friend from language school days who was working in southern Hokkaido, came to help us. The schoolhouse was crowded with almost every family in the district. We showed a film in Japanese about Helen Keller, a Biblical film and a travelogue on Canada. Since this was in the days before television the whole community was starved for entertainment of any kind. We made new friends and also informed them about the work of the Dohoku Centre and the Three Love School events we were holding for farmers. As a result several of the young people attended some of the sessions of the Three Love Schools.

As we got to know some of the pioneer farmers we learned that their lot was not an easy one. Hillside farms were not very productive and were limited in the range of crops they could grow. The area was most suited to dairy farming, but the plots they had been given were much too small to carry on financially viable dairy farms. Gradually most of the farmers sold their farms to their neighbours and moved away. Within a few years the school which had started out with 30 children was reduced to five students. The school was closed and the remaining children had to attend school in town.

HIROSHI HAENO

One of the farms that remained and prospered was that of the Haeno family. They built a house and dairy barn on a hillside near Nayoro and grew hay on most of the land which had belonged to the original pioneer community. The eldest son, Hiroshi, had an accident with a tractor that necessitated the amputation of one leg. However, he did not let this handicap stop him from farming. With an artificial leg, he continued to drive the tractor and do all the work involved in running a dairy farm with over fifty cows. After getting out of the hospital he attended Three Love Schools and came to the Dohoku Centre English School to learn English conversation. We had many close relationships with Hiroshi and his family.

A sequel to this story took place after Doreen and I had returned to Canada and were working in Fort Qu'Appelle, Saskatchewan at the Prairie Christian Training Centre. We received a letter from Hiroshi saying that he was getting married to Etsuko and for their honeymoon they would like to visit us in Canada. We wrote back that we would be delighted to have them as our guests. When they came we showed them the sights of the beautiful Qu'Appelle valley. One day we took them for a picnic in the Katepwa Lake Park. He had mentioned that he had heard of the thunderstorms of Saskatchewan and that he hoped he could witness one. On the day of our picnic, just as we were gathering up the remains of the picnic a big dark cloud appeared in the west over the lake. As we came out of the park and were driving along the lake, the rain started descending in sheets. We stopped the car and witnessed one of the most spectacular thunder and lightning storms that we had seen in the West. Hiroshi and Etsuko were exhilarated that they had really seen an authentic Saskatchewan thunderstorm.

6

NEW WAYS OF BEING CHURCH

One of the roles envisaged for the Dohoku Centre was to help coordinate the work of the churches in the northern area of Hokkaido. As new churches were being established and newly ordained ministers were sent to take over the work, a number of problems developed. The traditional pattern was for the mission of the church to be centred around the minister and each church was a separate entity. There was usually little communication between neighbouring churches and a lack of trained lay leadership. In addition to the churches that had been built there were also many "house churches" served with weekday meetings, first by Mr. Tamura and myself and later with the help of new ministers who were appointed to the newly built churches. However, there was little coordination in this work.

The new ministers who came were recent graduates from seminary, coming from southern parts of Japan. For them, living in Hokkaido was almost like coming to a foreign land. Customs were different and they were not used to the severe winters. The ministers and their young wives often became lonely and discouraged and decided to seek churches in warmer climates. After the arrival of Mitsuo Nakamura on the staff of the Dohoku Centre, we began to experiment with a new concept of "group ministry" and "larger parish mission" starting with the region surrounding Nayoro which we called the "Nayoro Larger Parish." Approximately once a week the ministers of Nayoro, Shimokawa, and Shibetsu met at the Dohoku Centre for fellowship, joint study, and program planning. We developed programmes for lay leaders' training and special events to bring the churches together several times a year. There were programmes for youth, women's groups and entire congregations. The new ministers found mutual support in the group ministry and in the joint events which brought the various congregations together.

One of the most successful of the joint events was a yearly memorial service held in the Nayoro church in early August at the same time as the Buddhist and other religious groups gathered for their memorial services. Since none of the other communities had a Christian burial ground, members from the other churches were invited to inter the ashes of their deceased members in the Nayoro Mausoleum in the Nayoro town cemetery. The first Sunday in August members from all the churches worshipped together in the Nayoro church. At this service the names of all Christian members who had died from the time of the founding of the churches were memorialized by the reading of their names and by prayers. After the service the congregation went to the cemetery for a further brief worship at the grave site. The whole group then returned to the church kindergarten for lunch and fellowship together. This yearly event unified the churches of the region more than any other.

One of the immediate effects of the group ministry program was that the ministers and their families began to remain in the churches for longer periods of time and the work became much more stabilized. A further advantage was that Christians and seekers in the isolated house churches also became part of a larger fellowship. The Nayoro Larger Parish covered an area about 100 kilometres long and 70 kilometres wide and soon came to include 6 churches and 4 house churches. The work of the parish was planned by the Larger Parish Committee which included the ministers of the area and several lay representatives from each of the churches. By 1967 the group ministry included, Rev. Yoshiya Sakurai, the new minister at Nayoro, Rev. Mitsuko Hosoumi, the minister of the Wassamu and Shibetsu churches, Rev. Motozo Ashizawa, minister of the Shimokawa and Okoppe churches, Mitsuo Nakamura and myself. Because of the success we had in the Nayoro Larger Parish we decided to expand our horizons and invite the churches in Asahigawa and the Wakkanai regions to explore the possibility of developing the whole of northern Hokkaido into larger parish regions. Joined by the Rev. Kawatani of the Roku-jo church in

Asahigawa and Rev. Ueno of the Wakkanai Church we began to study further the whole Larger Parish concept. Our study included a book by Marvin Judy, entitled *The Larger Parish and Group Ministry* and a booklet published by the United Church of Christ in Japan entitled "New Church Development." We also wrote a Lay Leaders' Training Course of five sessions which could be used both in the local churches and at the Dohoku Centre.

With the further involvement of lay leaders from the churches we developed the Northern Region Larger Parish plan. This plan included the dividing of the whole northern region of Hokkaido into three "larger parishes": the Asahigawa (southern region), the Nayoro (central region) and the Wakkanai (northern region). In addition to special joint programs among the churches of each region there were also several events a year planned for the three regions together. For these the facilities of the Dohoku Centre were sometimes too small in which case we met in a hot-springs hotel.

Another innovation was a yearly "pulpit exchange" among churches of the whole Northern Region. A roster was drawn up each year for the ministers to go to a church other than their own for Sunday service. In most cases a lay person would accompany the minister and assist in the presentation. This helped to further cement the relations between all the Kyodan churches in northern Hokkaido. In a report about the work of the Nayoro Larger Parish I wrote:

> The rate of growth of the churches in the area has not increased appreciably but all the churches have been kept alive and in four additional communities house meetings have been started with meetings once a month. There is a new spirit of hope among the members themselves.

In addition, as a part of a group ministry, I found a more defined role and a greater support for the work I was doing. One of the words of approbation for my work came from a member of the larger parish planning group who said, "We don't think of you as a foreigner any more but as one of us."

MARY ELLEN NETTLE

As the work of the Larger Parish in the northern region expanded a need was seen for leadership in Christian education, both in Sunday Schools for children and youth and for an expanded training for lay leaders. We applied for the appointment of Mary Ellen Nettle to head up this aspect of outreach throughout the whole northern region. Mary Ellen joined us in February of 1967.

Mary Ellen had taught high school in Canada for a time before going to the United Church Training School and then volunteering for service in Japan. After teaching English in Tokyo for several years she decided she would prefer to work more directly with the Japanese church. We greatly appreciated having a Canadian partner to assist in the work until June of 1968 at which time we left for Canada for a one year "home assignment." For the year we were away Mary Ellen continued the work along with a Japanese co-worker. While in Nayoro, Mary Ellen gave leadership, both in programmes of the Dohoku Centre and in churches throughout the region. Recently, Mary Ellen wrote about her experience:

> When I first attended a meeting of the Team ministers I was amazed at how well they worked and studied together. This was powerful. Present among that small group (four ministers and Floyd Howlett) was a strong sense of trust and co-operation as well as energy and eagerness to work together. In that part of Hokkaido where six feet of snow is normal, people need one another very much.
>
> My work was divided up in the following way: first and most important was the work with Church School teachers which I tried to do at meetings and in workshops to learn new ways of teaching children more effectively. The next part of my work was travelling with Miss Hosoumi who was the minister in the nearby town of Shibetsu. We often went out to make house calls and sometimes we held a "house

church" meeting. The most important was one with Miyaou Usui, a young man with a crippling condition of cerebral palsy. We often visited him and once the young people came to join a house church meeting. Miss Hosoumi and I worked well together and often as we returned home after a long day we stopped at the Osushi Bar to have a treat.

A third area of work was with English camps which were held in the winter school break and in the summer vacation time. It was a great opportunity for students to learn English conversation with a non-Japanese teacher. We were able to get teachers from among missionaries and also from the young men stationed at the Wakkanai US Air Base.

One winter we held a special event for young women to give them an opportunity to study together about family life and discuss their future expectations. Also, at that event there were special classes in flower-arranging, cooking and copper enamelling. There were a variety of other involvements such as visiting church schools or going to a public school for a special visit.

It was a privilege to work in the Team Ministry and I know I learned a great deal in those few years, one being to speak Japanese better than I had before. It was a great place to live and work and I cherish the memory of the place and the people.

After our return from Canada in 1969 Mary Ellen continued to work with us until the following spring. Working with her was a great inspiration and support. She made a valuable contribution through her training of church school leaders in all the churches in the Northern Hokkaido region. Her close association with the ministry of the Rev. Mistsuko Hosoumi in house churches and family visitation meant a great deal to Mitsuko and to the people they served together. Mary Ellen shared much of the burden with us and gave a great boost to our spirits. We missed her deeply when she left.

THE HOUSE CHURCH MOVEMENT

One of the decisions of the Northern Hokkaido Region planning committee was to expand the house church movement. We envisaged two types of "house churches." One was within towns where there was already an established church. These were planned as neighbourhood meetings to which friends could be invited for informal discussions and Bible study. The other type was for towns and villages where there was no church at all. We had already been doing these fairly successfully, but felt that with the assistance of trained lay leaders this programme could be expanded considerably.

We set out to train lay people for group leadership and more effective Bible study. We held two training sessions at the Dohoku Centre; a one day conference in September and a two day conference in November. We found that lay people were also eager to take more responsibility for leadership in the church. One lay person remarked: "The ministers are not the only ones who have a pipeline to God." The general theme of the two conferences was "Is the Church Alright the Way It Is?" (implying that changes were needed) with sub-themes of "What is the Place of Social Action in Today's Church?" and "What Is the Place of Lay People in Today's Church?" In answer to both of these questions there was an overwhelming consensus that the Bible called for all the "people of God," both clergy and lay, to be involved in issues of justice and human rights. A follow-up dialogue session, held with the ministers and the church board members of the northern region, was valuable for both the lay people and the ministers.

During the Christmas vacation the Dohoku Centre held a "Friends of the Bible" Conference for young people in co-operation with a Sapporo based "radio evangelism" program. Young people who had been listening to the radio Bible study sessions, as well as young people from the churches, participated in this conference. This was another opportunity to join in dialogue about the centrality of the Bible in daily life issues.

Seeing the need for a text on how to lead Bible study, Mitsuo Nakamura and myself translated an appendix to Alan Richardson's book *Preface to Bible Study*. This gives some practical suggestions on how to run Bible study groups, either with clergy or lay leaders. The study points out that the main purpose is not to flood the participants with Biblical knowledge, but to make the text deeply personal. It states:

> God speaks to us through the Bible in order that God may speak through us to others. Such study is a sharing of the truth which God has revealed to one member with all the other members of the group. . . What does this mean in practice? It means that every member of the group must come to grips with the question, 'What does this passage mean to me?' . . . It is in the effort to articulate one's own deepest convictions that one truly apprehends them for oneself.

This approach helped to make Bible study come alive and encouraged lay people to take leadership. Gradually, with more trained leaders, we were able to expand the number of "house meetings" and "house churches" in the northern region. At one time there were over 20 of these sessions being held once or twice a month with a wide variety of approaches.

One of the most innovative was a monthly meeting held in a copper-mining village in a mountain area near Shimokawa. The Hokkaido Board of Education had a policy of arbitrarily appointing teachers who had been teaching in city schools to serve in country schools for periods of 3 or 4 years. Koichi Saito, a Junior High School English teacher, his wife, Tamiko, and their two children received quite a shock to be sent from the City of Asahigawa to a small isolated school in the mountains. As the only Christians in the village they were very lonely. I agreed to go once a month for a meeting in their home. Koichi offered to lead the meeting with assistance from myself and any lay people I could bring from the Shimokawa church.

Koichi did not think the usual approach to Bible study of studying a Biblical text would work effectively in that community. He suggested that we invite people from the community and the school to meet for discussion and snack sessions. He proposed putting the agenda for each discussion in the hands of the participants. They would suggest a topic that was of interest to them for the next meeting. It might be education, politics, family life, children, human relations, or any other topic. Koichi led a discussion in a general way and then asked me, "Does the Bible have anything to say on topics like this?" I knew beforehand the topic that was to be discussed but I never knew the way in which the discussion would go. I could only prepare by thinking about possible directions. Of course Tamiko and Koichi also added from their knowledge of the Bible and Christian life. The group consisted of a number of other teachers, the school caretaker and some women friends that Tamiko had made in the community. There was always a lively discussion and also considerable interest in looking at a current issue from a faith basis.

These meetings could never be called a "house church," but they proved to be among the most effective study groups I can remember. The meetings stopped when the Saitos were moved back to Asahigawa, after they had served their four-year term in the hinterland. Another more typical "house church" was that which has been carried on for many years in the home of Noriyoshi Nishizaki in the village of Kenbuchi about 45 minutes south of Nayoro.

Noriyoshi grew up in Kenbuchi but when he went to Sapporo to train to become a postal worker, he started to go to church, taking part in the young peoples' group and becoming a Christian. When he went back to his hometown he discovered that he was the only Christian in his village. The Japanese ministers in the area and myself agreed to go to his home once a month for meetings with Noriyoshi and any of his neighbours and friends. A little group of six to eight people sat on the tatami floor around a low table. There was hymn singing, participatory Bible study, followed by tea and cookies. After a few years he was married, but his wife was not a Christian.

At first she did not sit down with the group, but remained in the kitchen preparing the tea and cookies. However, from the kitchen she was listening attentively and after about two years she joined the group. In a few years two lovely daughters were born and as they grew older they gathered some of their friends for a children's meeting with Bible stories and children's songs. When the daughters were about ten and twelve they decided that they wanted to be Christians like their father, and arrangements were made to go to the Shibetsu church for baptism. Their mother then declared, "If my daughters are going to be baptized I will too. In this way we can become a Christian family." Noriyoshi never tried to persuade his wife to become a Christian. He waited for her to make that decision on her own.

There was never any thought that we could build a church in Kenbuchi. Although a few young people who attended the "house church" did also become Christians, they all moved away and the regular attendance never grew beyond six or eight. The Kenbuchi house church is just one example of similar groups that have persisted for thirty or forty years.

The pattern set by the northern Hokkaido churches of house churches and Bible study groups has been picked up by other churches in the rest of Hokkaido as an effective means of Christian outreach. The main body of the United Church of Christ was also impressed by the house church movement in Hokkaido and sent a leader from Tokyo to study the activity.

NAYORO-LINDSAY TWINNING

The Dohoku Centre was founded with the vision that it was to serve, not only the church but the whole community. The opportunity to do this came when the city of Nayoro began to consider the possibility of linking with an overseas city in a twinning relationship. When Mitsuo Nakamura heard of this proposal he approached Mayor Kotaro Ikeda with the suggestion that a suitable city might be found in Canada.

In the spring of 1969 while we were on home assignment in Canada we received a letter from Mayor Ikeda asking us to recommend a Canadian town that might like to enter into a twinning relationship with Nayoro. Doreen immediately thought of her home town of Lindsay. The Mayor of Lindsay, John Eakins, was a friend with whom she had grown up in school and church. We approached John and he was enthusiastic. He took the proposal to the town council where it was unanimously approved. Word was sent back to Japan and the Nayoro City Council agreed to twin with Lindsay. Joint celebrations were held in Nayoro and Lindsay on August 1st, 1969, shortly before our return to Japan.

In Lindsay, a "twinning ceremony" was held in Victoria Park with the attendance of the Japan Consul General from Toronto. Dr. Bill Service, a local surgeon who had grown up in China as the son of missionary parents, was chosen as the Chair of the Lindsay Twinning organizing Committee.

The launching of the Sister Relationship was the beginning of a friendship that has now lasted over thirty years and has involved hundreds of citizens of both cities in exchange visits. One of the first of these were official visits by the two mayors.

In April of 1970 John Eakins, his wife Iris and the McElroys made the first official visit from Lindsay to Nayoro. There was a huge welcoming dinner with speeches and gifts. As part of the program, the guests and ourselves were asked to sing a typical Canadian song. Not being trained singers we chose "I've Been Working on the Railroad" with Doreen giving the accompaniment on a wind-blown keyboard. The Japan Defence Corps band which was in attendance immediately picked up the tune and joined in to the merriment of the assembled crowd. When all the Nayoro participants were invited to shake hands with the Lindsay guests, we noticed several getting in the line twice so that they could repeat the hand-shake.

We welcomed the Eakins and McElroys into our home and accompanied them on the many visits they made to city locations. One of the most meaningful was to an elementary school, made at the specific request of John Eakins. Students were overjoyed to ask questions and join in folk dancing with the mayors of both towns.

One evening the Nayoro Twinning Committee met with the Lindsay delegation to talk about future plans. One of the proposals was for student exchanges between the two towns. This plan was implemented in 1972 when Cathy Jackson from Lindsay and Yuriko Oikawa from Nayoro exchanged visits. Subsequently two from each town were exchanged in alternate years. Up until the year 2001, 24 high school students from Lindsay and 20 students from Nayoro had participated in this project. For those who took part, the one month visit overseas was a life changing experience. One outstanding example was that of Mark Hamilton, a 1987 exchange student.

Mark fell in love with a beautiful Japanese girl, and in the summer of 2000, I, along with an official exchange group from Lindsay, were privileged to be present at their wedding at the Nayoro shrine, during our visit celebrating the 31st anniversary of the Twinning. The high school student exchange has been one of the most meaningful and fruitful results of the twinning relationship.

An extension of the high school student exchange took place a few years later when the Nayoro Junior College requested an opportunity for students from the college to come to Lindsay on study tours. For many years, two students from the college have come to Lindsay for several weeks, to do research on children's education, nutrition and other college-related topics.

The visit to Nayoro by John and Iris Eakins was followed by the visit of the Nayoro Mayor Kotaro Ikeda and his wife to Lindsay. The town of Lindsay put on a tremendous welcome for the Ikedas and the group accompanying them. An interesting sidelight to this visit was a phone call Doreen received from Mrs. Ikeda on her return. She remarked how grateful she was for the fact that Mayor Eakins had brought his wife with him for the formal visit to Nayoro. Having John's wife accompany him had obligated Nayoro to send her along to Lindsay, something that otherwise might not have happened according to Japanese custom. Mrs. Ikeda was completely overwhelmed by the reception they had received. This was just one indication of the way in which the twinning relationship began to break down the gender divide that is traditional in Japanese society.

At the time of the implementation of the twinning the one negative voice that came from the Lindsay community was from the Canadian Legion, some of whose members were reported to have remarked, "Why do we want to link up with Japan, a country with which we were at war, and about which we have heard so many atrocity stories?" However, at the time of the visit of the second Lindsay Mayor, David and Pam Logan, a Lindsay town Council member, Tom Madill and his wife Edna were part of the entourage. Tom had been the President of the Legion, and had rather hesitantly joined the party. After four days of celebration and a huge final banquet with many of the Nayoro citizens, Tom came back to our house and exclaimed, "When I get back, I'll have to tell those boys that its not like they think it is." He must have done a good job convincing Legion members of the sincerity of the Japanese people, since the next summer, when we happened to be back in Canada, Lindsay was visited by a Nayoro delegation of 20 people. We found that the welcoming party for the Nayoro delegation was held in the Legion Hall with the Legion ladies doing the catering. By that demonstration we surmised that the last shreds of prejudice against the Japanese people had evaporated.

In 1981, on the occasion of our departure from Nayoro, thirty years after first coming to Japan, the city of Nayoro presented Doreen and myself with a framed plaque with the following message printed in Japanese and English:

> Together, you have given of yourselves greatly to establish, maintain and develop the sister city relationship between Nayoro and Lindsay. Together, you have given Nayoro citizens a broader international perspective and have contributed to raising the cultural level of our city. Your achievement has truly been great. In recognition of your achievement and to express our friendship, respect and gratitude to both of you, I as Mayor of Nayoro, Japan, and representing the people of Nayoro, hereby make you honorary citizens of international goodwill, of Nayoro, and grant you freedom of the city.
>
> Signed by Yoshio Ishikawa,
Mayor of Nayoro City, Japan.

Doreen and I were filled with an overwhelming sense of gratitude for this recognition of the years we had spent in Nayoro. We were especially grateful that these words of appreciation were coming, not just from the church, but from the whole town.

ROB AND KEIKO WITMER

Rob and Keiko Witmer became the successors to the work of Doreen and myself when we left to return to Canada in June 1981, and are still continuing with amazing success when this is being written in the spring of 2002. Theirs is a fascinating story. I first met Rob Witmer in 1969 at Westminster College, London when Doreen and I were co-ordinating the orientation for new overseas mission personnel. We were back in Canada on home assignment and Rob, newly graduated in Arts from Queen's University, Kingston, was one of the appointees to Japan of the United Church Division of World Outreach.

The orientation course at that time was a comprehensive training programme that included studies in the theology and practice of mission, an introduction to the culture and politics of the various countries to which people were being sent, and preparation for dealing with the culture shock of living and working in a foreign environment. Dr. Katherine Hockin, the knowledgeable and experienced director of Ecumenical Forum, was the house theologian, and our mentor and guide.

We were impressed by the way in which Rob enthusiastically entered into the programme and by his eagerness to get to Japan. We were most delighted that he was appointed to teach at the Hokusei Women's College in Sapporo in Hokkaido, which meant that we could see him frequently. Rob lived with a Japanese family, applied himself and soon became quite fluent in Japanese.

We often welcomed him to Nayoro on weekends and during the Christmas holiday seasons. He soon became close friends with our children, Dennis, Peter and Susan and with Gordon Morwood who had come to teach English in the Dohoku Centre English School. Rob and Gord, both accomplished musicians and good folk vocalists, joined up with a Japanese musician friend, Morio Sasaki, and soon became a popular singing group in town. While he was teaching in Sapporo, Rob met Keiko who was taking kindergarten teacher's training there. Their meeting was quite coincidental. Rob had agreed to go with the director of a Hokkaido radio evangelism project to a church in the Hidaka peninsula region that just happened to be Keiko's home church. They met for the first time in the car going to her church at the tip of the Hidaka peninsula. Back in Sapporo their friendship blossomed and by the time Rob's three year term was drawing to a close they decided that they wanted to get married. However, they faced a huge road-block, for although Keiko's mother was in favour, her father was adamantly opposed to his daughter marrying a foreigner. They came to our house together to discuss their options. Much as they wanted to marry they decided that for the time being they would go along with her father's wishes with the hope that he would eventually change his mind. This meant that Rob had to return to Canada without Keiko. However, to everyone's surprise shortly after Rob had returned to Canada her father relented and said, "If you really want to marry Rob that much you can go to Canada and marry him there." Both of them were overjoyed. On landing in Vancouver she ran into another difficulty; she was stopped by Immigration since she had no return ticket to Japan and was suspected of trying to immigrate to Canada illegally. Rob had planned that they would fly back together on a joint ticket after they were married. Keiko was really bewildered. She tried to phone Rob in Goderich, but could only reach his mother. Keiko's English was limited and of course his mother didn't understand a word of Japanese. Keiko did manage to communicate that she had been stopped in Vancouver. When Rob returned he contacted Keiko through some friends in Vancouver who helped to clear up the misunderstanding, took her in over night, and sent her on to meet Rob in Toronto.

A few weeks later they were married on a beach near Goderich on a beautiful sunny day. After a short holiday and home assignment in Canada they flew back to Hokkaido in May of

1975 where, to our great joy, they were assigned to work in Nayoro while we went to Canada on home assignment during 1975-76. They moved into the mission house, our house. Manna, their first child, was born in Nayoro in April of 1976 while we were still in Canada. After we got back to Japan in September they continued to work with us until June of 1977 when Rob enrolled in Emmanuel College, Toronto to study theology. After ordination in May of 1980 they returned to Nayoro to again work with us until we returned to Canada to stay in May of 1981.

Although I had not yet reached retirement age we felt that with Rob and Keiko on hand to take over the work that this was an appropriate time to leave. We knew that the work was in very capable hands. Doreen had not fully recovered from an operation several years previously, and we felt that before retirement we would like to work a few years in the church in Canada.

One plan the Witmers developed after we left was forging a link between farm people in Hokkaido connected with the Three Love Programme and the Rural Life Committee of the London Conference of the United Church of Canada, Rob's Canadian church home district. Several fruitful exchanges of visitors have been made over the years.

These mutual exchanges have had a deep impact on the lives of the participants from both countries. Rob and Keiko need to be commended on their vision and enthusiasm for opening doors and new visions of mutual opportunities for solidarity between farm people of Hokkaido and Canada.

7

ENGAGEMENT WITH SOCIAL & POLITICAL ISSUES

One of the hopes we had in going to Japan was that by working with the church in Japan we could become agents of social change for a more peaceful and just society. This is not an easy task for a foreigner to undertake. As guests of the country we were prohibited from direct political action. Before the war some missionaries were at times monitored fairly closely. Fortunately for us, the post-war situation was much different. Peace education and peace demonstrations were being carried on quite openly by the Japanese themselves. All we had to do was to support their peace activities.

Every year there have been massive anti-nuclear and anti-war rallies in Hiroshima which had their birth in the holocaust of the atom-bombing of Hiroshima and Nagasaki. For instance, on August 6th, 1981, an anniversary of the bombing, over 60,000 people gathered in Hiroshima to protest the nuclear arms race and to call for a nuclear weapons free world. All over Japan there were teach-ins and rallies on the danger of the revival of militarism and calls to preserve the Peace Constitution.

For some time Japanese militarists kept a low profile, but in the late seventies and early eighties right wing groups began to make their voices heard. Huge black buses with powerful loud speakers blaring out military music appeared in the large cities of Japan. The haranguing voices urged the citizens to a greater willingness to defend the country, and called upon them to give a greater devotion to the Emperor.

Up until the June 1980 elections few people paid attention to the ravings of the far-right groups because the opposition political parties were able to put some restraint on the Liberal-Democratic party's plans for military expansion. But after the Liberal-Democrats won an absolute majority, the government began to push ahead on military arms build-up and through clever propaganda began to try to erode Japan's nuclear "allergy" and commitment to peace.

The church in Japan was quick to condemn the re-militarization of Japan. In July of 1981, the Moderator of the United Church of Christ in Japan issued a statement to the church that said, "Because I sense the same trend of the times as forty years ago on the eve of World War II, I feel constrained to say something to the church today." He urged the church not to make the mistake it had made before in approving the country's march into war, but as part of its confession of Jesus as Lord, to fulfill its responsibilities to build peace in Japan and the world.

The Nayoro church, in cooperation with the Dohoku Centre, was active in peace education. Every year on the February 11th "National Foundation Day" we organized peace study sessions and on August 15th, the anniversary of the end of World War II, we had outdoor marches and rallies to recall the horrors of war and protest military build-up. These events were organized by the church but also involved labour union groups, the Socialist Party, the Communist party and any other community organizations that would participate. For instance, On February 11th, 1981 over 200 people gathered in the civic auditorium to hear a lecture by the Rev. Sanae Hashimoto, a peace activist from Sapporo, speak on the Emperor-system and the dangers of re-militarization. There were no overt movements on the part of the government to prohibit these actions.

By 1980, however, not only were the right wing parties in Japan calling for re-militarization but the U.S. government, which had urged the "Peace Constitution" on Japan in the first place, was now urging Japan to re-arm, and incidentally to buy more planes and weapons from the U.S. Incensed by this foreign pressure, in March 1981 the annual Kyodan-Related Missionary Conference of over 100 missionaries from the U.S. and Canada, the last missionary conference I attended, sent a petition to President Reagan protesting the call for arms build-up.

THE HIROSHIMA IMPACT

The devastating effects of the atomic bombing of Hiroshima and Nagasaki were one of the main factors fuelling the Japanese peace movement. Peace activists were determined that no other nation would ever have to endure the horror they had experienced.

Although I had heard much and read a great deal about Hiroshima and Nagasaki, the full impact of the holocaust caused by the bombing did not really hit me until I visited Hiroshima in the spring of 1981, shortly before returning to Canada. There I saw the children's memorial, draped with strings of paper cranes representing the prayers of children from all over Japan and the world that peace might prevail.

Then, as I stood before the huge memorial mound containing the ashes of thousands of unknown dead, I offered up a prayer committing myself, on my return to Canada, to give priority to activities for peace. This commitment was confirmed by a phone call I received the day after we arrived back in Toronto. The call was from Setsuko Thurlow, a survivor of Hiroshima and a close friend, inviting us to a peace meeting at her home the next evening. Since then I have made work for peace through the Canadian Project Ploughshares peace movement a major thrust of all my social justice activities in Canada.

THE "BONSAI" EDUCATIONAL SYSTEM

During the sixties and seventies we observed a number of disturbing trends in government policies with respect to the educational system. One of these trends was a gradual tightening of control over education. Whereas, in the immediate post-war period there had been a flowering of democracy with locally elected school boards, and a greater freedom on the part of teachers to develop innovative curriculum, gradually the government took over and instituted centrally directed authoritarian control.

Elected school boards were abolished, and directors of education and school boards were appointed by the government. Teachers' unions had grown in strength and at times challenged the government on some of its policies, so the government set out to emasculate the unions. Whereas Principals and Vice-Principals had been part of the union, they were given management roles along with the directors of education with responsibility of enforcing stricter rules. School texts were revised to cut out criticisms of the war and to foster patriotism. Teachers were told to teach only what was on the government-mandated curriculum and open discussion of government policies or social problems was prohibited. Teachers who did not cooperate could arbitrarily be banished to isolated rural schools.

Along with these policies, because of the fierce competition for students to get into the more prestigious universities, the main goal of education became the ability to pass examinations. To try to compete, parents sent their children to extra classes after school hours in private schools. Often during summer and winter vacations students were sent to special schools teaching them how to cram for examinations. This has made for what has been labelled "examination hell." Some students who developed mental problems even committed suicide.

Shortly before returning to Canada in 1981 I was asked by the Nayoro Teachers College to give a talk to the entire teaching staff and student body on my assessment of the educational system in Japan. This was an opportunity I couldn't pass up. I pulled no punches. I told them that the system as I saw it was what I called "bonsai education." Japanese education could be compared to the way in which Japanese gardeners cut and control the roots and branches of dwarf trees until they grow and develop to produce just the kind of "bonsai" tree they want. I said that in the same way it seemed to me that Japanese educational authorities were trying to develop a system that would educate students into the industrial system that the government and the corporate sector demanded. I regretted that the schools did not promote free thought or aim to develop well-rounded individuals. I was afraid that I would receive some criticism from the educators, but they congratulated me and agreed that there was a lot in what I had said. I sensed that most of the professors felt that they too were caught in the system.

At the Dohoku Centre through our English conversation camps we tried to counteract some of the damage done in the school. Although daytime classes were spent in English conversation, evenings were spent discussing, in Japanese, issues of concern to the students - issues of school policy, with opportunities for open discussion of social and political problems that were prohibited in the schools. We always hoped that we were something of a subversive influence on the educational system. One of the difficulties we ran into, however, was that, with many of the best students being forced to go to cram schools during the summer, fewer and fewer students were able to participate in our summer programmes.

Having seen the detrimental results of this kind of educational policy in Japan makes me all the more apprehensive about the changes taking place in educational policies in Ontario. The denigrating of teachers, the stress on standard examinations, the under funding of education, the stress on a core curriculum with a downgrading of the arts and the increasing top-down control makes me fear for the future of education here in Canada as well. Here too, the system is already producing graduates whose primary goal is getting well paying jobs and who lack a critical analysis.

RURAL COOPERATIVES

Another area of concern was what we saw happening to the farmers' cooperatives in Japan. The rural cooperatives, which had been started by Dr. Toyohiko Kagawa, had become one of the most comprehensive cooperative movements in the world. One of the major study topics of our Three Love Schools were rural co-ops. Here, as in the educational system, we saw a democratic cooperative movement being eroded by authoritarian government control. Whereas, for years almost every farm community was organized into locally directed cooperatives, the government began to force amalgamation of neighbouring cooperatives so that control became further removed from local communities. In the cities large central Co-op stores were set up that became not much different from commercial supermarkets or private corporations.

One of the aims of the Three Love Schools was to discuss with the young people the directions the cooperatives were taking, encouraging the participants to go back to their own communities determined to work for local control and the preservation of the essential nature of the cooperative movement.

Many of the graduates did return to their own communities and eventually were elected as directors of their local co-ops. The cooperative movement in Japan is still strong but it requires continual vigilance on the part of rural communities to maintain the cooperative movements' core principles and vision.

POLITICAL AND ECONOMIC ANALYSIS

Another goal of the Three Love Schools was to give the participants the tools for political and economic analysis. Professor Ota, of the Nopporo Agricultural College, was of great assistance in accomplishing this goal. He was a dedicated Christian with a strong social consciousness. He gave lectures and led discussions on the political, economic and social issues facing farmers in Japan. Professor Ota spoke out vehemently against the policies of the governing Liberal Democratic Party that he said was neither liberal nor democratic. He criticised the increasing power of the corporate monopolies that were amalgamating and gaining control of much of the economy. He warned of the danger of the revival of nationalistic militarism. For many of the farm young people coming from conservative rural communities, his presentations were a stimulus to more progressive political action when they returned home.

COMMUNITY SOCIAL OUTREACH

One of the goals we had when building the Dohoku Centre was to reach out into the broader community, responding to its felt needs. An opportunity to do this came through Dr. Toyoji Kumagai, a psychiatrist at the local city hospital and a board member of the Dohoku Centre. He was painfully aware of the failings of the Japanese medical system with regard to the needs of people with mental illness who were warehoused in the psychiatric wards of hospitals. Dr. Kumagai ended up trying to care for a far greater number than it was possible to do effectively. He was also frustrated by the fact that even after the patients were well on the way to recovery many families would not accept them back. He saw a tremendous need for a "halfway" house where patients could be given assistance in re-entering society.

We became personally involved in the need for a support network for people with mental health problems, as we welcomed some of Dr. Kumagai's patients into our home on Sunday afternoons. In the year before our return to Canada, working in cooperation with Dr. Kumagai, the Dohoku Centre approached the Hokkaido Prefectural government to try to secure funds to build such a much-needed centre. The government recognized the need, but said there was no money for such a project. The implementation was left to our successors, Rob and Keiko Witmer, along with Yoshiro Kishimoto, who came on staff as the Co-director of the Dohoku Centre in 1978, to bring the dream into fruition. Even before the Centre could get any government support they started a pilot project, accommodating six persons recovering from mental illness, within the existing facilities of the Centre.

Yoshiro Kishimoto had a special interest in this project because a member of his family had been stricken with mental illness. In a Dohoku Centre news bulletin, Yoshiro Kishimoto wrote:

> At the same time as we seek to enable the mentally ill to achieve a new independence, we also want to work towards the creation of a community of warm human relationships where all are accepted and seek to live together.

After several years, when the pilot project had proven its value, funds became available from the Hokkaido government to build a new facility on the Dohoku Centre grounds with accommodation for twenty people. It also had facilities for a sheltered workshop that served not only residential members, but also those who were living in the community.

Recently, a new venture has been the establishment of a "daily life support room," a drop in centre in town, to which anyone can come for refreshments, talk and mutual help. To support these new community service projects a new independent board made up of the "Nayoro District Family Association of Persons with Mental Illness" was formed. All these new facilities serve the function of social rehabilitation and participation. This is another way in which the Dohoku Centre and the Nayoro church has sought to fulfill its mission of becoming the church in the world.

OPPOSITION TO BUILDING THE NARITA AIRPORT

In 1966 the government of Japan decided to build a new airport that eventually became the Narita International Airport. Part of the land required was crown land belonging to the Emperor. However, in addition, a huge area would have to be bought or expropriated from farmers, many of whom had been living in the region for generations on some of the best agricultural land in the country. The struggle of these farmers to prevent the takeover of their land went on for eleven years before the first plane took off from the new airport. This is an epic story of resistance in post-war Japan.

The farmers' main struggle took place around the village of Sanrizuka. Without a single consultation with local residents the government announced they were taking over the required area. In post-war Japan there was a particularly strong national longing for truly democratic governance. The entire nation had been devastated and demoralized by the war, so a continuation of autocratic behaviour on the part of government was not going to be tolerated by the people. I think it was both sympathy with the plight of the farmers and a reaction against authoritarianism that mobilized many thousands of supporters in the Sanrizuka struggle.

The government's offer to pay compensation or provide land elsewhere for the affected farmers caused a division between those who agreed to negotiate with the government and those who refused. A large proportion of area residents adamantly refused to move no matter what they were offered. This triggered a series of confrontations which continued for over eleven years.

In the first expropriation struggle, in 1971, 1,500 farmers from the region plus 2,500 supporters from the rest of the nation gathered to resist both government and the Airport Authority. They built strongholds and dug "suicide tunnels" into which older men and women crawled, daring the bulldozers to begin the work of levelling the land. They chained themselves to trees so the only way they could be dislodged was cutting down the trees with the protesters in them. The Airport Authority sent in 18,000 riot police and 200 bulldozers and boasted they could, "take care of the situation in four hours." In fact it took 14 days just to dislodge them. Over 1,000 protestors were wounded by the police and 400 arrested in this incident alone.

The Airport Authority did finally "secure" their area and one runway was completed in January of 1978. However, just prior to the official opening of the airport, a 62 metre tall iron tower, built on a high solid cement foundation, in an almost inaccessible location, appeared at the end of the runway! The opposition coalition claimed responsibility for the tower, and announced their intention to defend it. The Airport Authority had to build a road to gain access to the tower and prepared to take over the tower with thousands of riot police. This time, beginning on April 17th, over 23,000 supporters from all over the country participated in a "Rally to Fight for the Iron Tower." When the riot police attacked, 327 people were injured. Not until May 6th was the Airport Authority able to dislodge the protestors and demolish the tower. For almost five months the Narita Airport with all its facilities in place was completely unusable. This was an amazing victory for the farmers and protestors.

The determination of the farmers to protect their land was indomitable. In Kikujiro Fukushima's book, *Report From A Battle Field, Sanrizuka, 1967-1977*, the Vice-Chairman of the Airport Opposition League, Seiji Ishibashi, who owned a house in which four generations of his family lived, had this to say about their struggle:

> The government and the Corporation are expropriating our land without consulting us. They are trampling on the right of the farmers to protect their own land, arresting people indiscriminately, terrorizing people. They are the ones who created the Sanrizuka struggle. I will never forgive them.

Initially our involvement in the struggle was only peripheral. From Hokkaido we could only watch the saga from the sidelines, albeit with intense interest. It was not until after the completion of the first runway that our family got involved.

It happened that our eldest son, Dennis, who was living in Canada at that time, came back to Japan for an Asian Justice and Peace Conference. One place they visited was Sanrizuka, the centre of the farmers' resistance movement. Dennis served as translator for the Justice and Peace group whose members came from many Asian countries.

Our other two children, Peter and Susan, were living in Tokyo and began to go to the solidarity hut, which served as hostel and fortress against expected attacks. On weekends students from the city went out to Sanrizuka to support the farmers by assisting in work on the farms, hoeing, gathering produce and giving moral support to the tiny remaining band of farmers. Susan kept a journal of her experiences. Here are excerpts from her journal:

> When we go, we stay at the "Worker-Farmer Unity Hut" - a sort of bunk house. During the day we work on farms, mostly vegetable farms. We work in the fields with the family, eat lunch, supper and have a bath and then sit around a small table on the floor, drinking tea and talking. They are an amazing people. One farmer was telling me how at first, 13 years ago, they fought to protect their private land. But over the years, as they came into direct contact with government officials, the court systems, etc., and contradictions became clear, they saw they were fighting for far more than just their private land. It was a fight of people refusing to let large development projects which serve the needs of big business (and military) and the government, push them aside.
>
> Farmers in Japan have always been near the bottom as far as social and economic status and most have

an inferiority complex. This has completely changed now. Another change is in the role of women. Whenever there was a village meeting, it used to be that only the men would go. Now, all the farm women go because they are, as one farmer's son put it, "half the force." The men say that often the women are tougher when it comes to resisting riot police.

When we saw how our own children were involved, Doreen and I decided to visit Sanrizuka ourselves to better understand the situation and give support to Susan and Peter and the farmers. While in Tokyo for a spring missionary conference we took the opportunity to worship in the little United Church of Christ in Japan congregation in Sanrizuka. One of the lay people in this church was Issaku Tomura, a metal worker who produced beautiful metal sculptures. Issaku was one of the leaders of the local opposition movement. After the church service he took us around to some of the sites of their struggle. He drove us to the site of the famous "Iron Tower." All that remained now was the solid cement base. We were shown the hostel/fortress with its solid door and heavy trap-door to the second storey to deter any attacking force. The airport was guarded by armed police continually circling the perimeter of the airport in armoured buses. It was a little scary for us when one of these patrols stopped the car and began questioning Issaku. We left without incident, but it gave us a sense of the kind of oppression which the local people felt all the time. We were proud of our children for their involvement in the struggle.

The opening of the Narita airport was not the end of the struggle. In August of 1977 the Airport Corporation had announced it was going to build a second runway. On the site of this construction there were still twenty-three farm families who had not given up the struggle.

Because of the continuing opposition the second runway has not yet been built twenty four years later. Patrols still guard the airport perimeter and all travellers who use the Narita Airport must pay an extra "security tax" on top of their ticket.

RELATIONS WITH THE POLICE AND LOCAL AUTHORITIES

Although some of our programmes at the Dohoku Centre could have been interpreted as anti-government, for the most part we experienced no interference. From time to time I was able to be of service to the police department when foreigners who spoke no Japanese came to town. I can only think of two occasions when we realised that we were "under surveillance."

The first incident had a connection to the airport struggle. In 1978 Yoshiro Kishimoto came on the staff of the Dohoku Centre as Co-director. Shortly after Yoshiro arrived we began getting visits at the Centre from two plain-clothes police. They were always very polite and showed an interest in the activities of the Centre. We wondered for a time what these visits were all about, until Yoshiro went to Osaka to visit his parents. I got a phone call from one of the police officers enquiring as to Yoshiro's whereabouts. At the time of the Sanrizuka airport struggles Yoshiro had been one of the student activists arrested for his participation in the protests. Because he supposedly had a "criminal record" for that activity, the police were keeping track of his whereabouts. I replied that he had gone to visit his parents, that he was an excellent citizen and worker. I also added that we didn't appreciate their visits to the Centre and that I hoped these would stop. They may have kept their eyes on us, but they never came back again.

The second incident involving the police took place at the time of the 1976 G-7 Summit Conference in Tokyo. Leaders of the seven major industrial nations met to discuss world trade. Security was tight throughout the whole nation. Doreen and I decided to take a few days rest at a small Japanese inn in Hamatombetsu, on the eastern coast of the Sea of Okhotsk. We settled in to the inn and then decided to go for a walk on the beautiful sandy beach. We had just got down to the beach when a car stopped on the road and two well-dressed men came down to meet us. We discovered that they were plain-clothes officers out to check our credentials. In Japan there is a requirement that all foreigners carry a "foreign registration card" and that they carry it with them at all times. Neither Doreen nor I had our cards with us at the beach. The officers said they would go back with us to the inn to get them. When we got back to the inn Doreen found her card but I remembered I had left the card in another pair of trousers. I did, however, have my Japanese driver's license. Doreen showed her card and they took down all the details. I showed them my driver's license and explained that I had left the card and asked, "Isn't the driver's license adequate to prove my identity?" However, they replied that they had to have the official card. They asked if we could phone back to Nayoro and have someone bring it to us. We explained that the children were away in Tokyo and there was no one at home. They then wanted us to drive back and get it. That would have meant a three hour trip there and back. I objected, saying that we had just come away for a quiet weekend and weren't going back for two days.

They then asked me to go with them to the Hamatombetsu police station. I said if they wanted to check my identity they could phone the Nayoro mayor. Instead they phoned the Nayoro police station who told them they knew me well. They finally agreed that if I took my registration card to the Nayoro police on my return they would accept that. They also insisted that I write an apology for not having my card with me and promise never to be without it again.

I learned afterwards that our missionary friends in Sapporo had also been visited by the police, so it looked as if all foreigners in Japan were being checked at the time of the Summit. The Japan security system may be more hidden but it is still in place.

8

DOREEN'S UNIQUE TALENTS

Up to this point I have talked mostly of my life odyssey in Japan and Canada, and have only incidentally referred to Doreen's role. I believe that the story of her important contributions needs a chapter by itself. How I wish that Doreen could tell her own story, but sadly, three years after our retirement in Lakefield, Doreen died. It is left to me to tell her story and pay tribute to her unique talents. One of her most outstanding talents was in expressing love for people. Her love enfolded myself and the children, but also extended to everyone she met both in Canada and in Japan. Her love overcame the natural reserve of the Japanese people and called forth a depth of affection from many of her friends there that was most unusual.

EARLY LIFE AND EXPERIENCES
Doreen grew up in Lindsay, Ontario, where her father William Agnew had been superintendent of the Sunday School and Adult Sunday School class teacher at Queen St. United Church. Doreen was active in the local young peoples' group, sang in the choir and was assistant pipe-organist. She was also a leader in the Presbytery and Conference Young Peoples' organizations. While attending the United Church Training School (sometimes humourously called "the Angel Factory"), where women were trained in Christian education leadership, she was a member of the College based Young Peoples' Forward Movement. This organization related faith to action, especially emphasizing the global responsibility of the church. It had been through the work of the Young Peoples' Forward Movement that some years earlier Doreen and I had met.

The Young Peoples' Forward Movement had a policy of sending out teams of students during the summer months to visit church camps and young peoples' groups. In the summer of 1943 my Victoria College roommate Morley Clarke and I were chosen to be the summer team and were sent out to travel throughout the United Church Bay of Quinte Conference in eastern Ontario. After completing some meetings in Peterborough, Loretta McDougall, the organizer of our meetings there remarked, "When you get to Lindsay, you'll be meeting Doreen, the organizer of your meetings there, she's a wonderful person, you'll enjoy meeting her." Immediately I was intrigued.

As President of the United Church Lindsay Presbytery Young Peoples' Union, Doreen was in charge of our itinerary for visiting churches in the Lindsay region. We stayed in her home in Lindsay and she accompanied us on our travels. Doreen told me years later of an incident that occurred as we started out on our Lindsay area itinerary. Morley and I were travelling in a Ford coupe with a "rumble seat." Doreen and a girl friend climbed into the front seat with Morley who was driving, and I got into the rumble seat by myself. Afterwards, her mother chided her, "Why did you leave Floyd sitting in the rumble seat all by himself?" It seems that she had immediately liked me and was a bit of a match-maker. I always appreciated "mother Agnew's" affection.

Later in the summer, Doreen and I met again when we both attended the Oak Lake Young People's Camp. During the following year we corresponded from time to time. The next summer Morley and I were again giving leadership at the Oak Lake Camp and Doreen was also there. That summer the Rev. Floyd Honey was the theme speaker. Floyd Honey's challenge at that camp was one of the major turning points in Doreen's life that led her to consider training for full time Christian service. Floyd Honey later volunteered as a missionary to China. After being evacuated from China because of the communist takeover, he was appointed as the East Asia Secretary of the United Church Division of World Mission and later as its General Secretary. This meant that when we went to Japan he also became our close personal friend and had general oversight of our mission endeavours.

At the Oak Lake Camp Floyd Honey spoke with passion about the joys of Christian service and the need for more Christian workers both in Canada and overseas. Doreen was tremendously moved and shared with me her desire to make a break from the secretary's job she was doing for her father's insurance firm and to prepare herself for some other form of ministry. In several long talks I encouraged her to enroll in the United Church Training School. She followed up on that suggestion and enrolled that fall. On the last night of camp Doreen and I sat by a tree in a secluded part of the camp and shared some of our hopes and dreams. We discovered that we had so much in common. As we parted I had a tremendous urge to give her a big hug and kiss, but at the last moment I restrained myself. I know young people today would think me an awful prude, but to me, at that time, a kiss was an act of commitment and I wasn't ready for that yet.

Doreen enrolled in the United Church Training School that fall, the same year I started at Emmanuel College. During the next two years we had frequent dates. We had many meaningful talks, but for some reason or other I still kept a wall of resistance between us. Somehow, I still found it hard to make a commitment and did not want to lead her on farther than I was prepared to go. We did develop a really close friendship and had long conversations about life and work but not about love.

SERVICE IN ORVILLE
Doreen graduated in 1947, after a two year course, a year before my graduation from Emmanuel College, and was appointed as minister to the Orville pastoral charge, near Parry Sound, which she had served as a summer student minister the year before. This appointment, in itself, was most unusual. She had so endeared herself to the people of those congregations that they had sent in a special petition to church headquarters asking that she be appointed for the full year - something that was unprecedented, since this was considered a "summer mission field." Doreen was persistent. She refused to accept any other appointment, She was overjoyed when she finally did get the appointment, and went back to live with Myrtle Ditchburn with whom she had formerly boarded. Myrtle lived in a tiny house with one extra guest room. She ran the local country

phone switchboard and knew everybody on her switchboard lines. On stormy days or nights when Doreen was out travelling Myrtle would follow her route by asking people on her phone lines if they had seen Doreen driving by safely.

Her old Ford car, which she named Gabriel, took her over some terrible winter roads in -30 to -40 degree temperatures. Since the car had no heater, her father lent her his old bearskin coat. She told the story of children being astounded to see what looked like a bear driving a car through a snow storm. She held services in six different towns and visited in many isolated homes in widely separated communities.

During that year we kept in contact frequently by letter. She shared stories of her experiences and of the visits to many lonely people. I will let her tell of one event that demonstrates the kind of love she expressed and the joy she brought to many people there:

> I called to see a dear old lady of 84 who had been in bed since Christmas. She had raised her two grandchildren, a girl of about 20 and a man of nearly 40. They insisted that I stay for tea. They were so glad to have the company, for both the old lady and the girl find it lonely, isolated as they are. They live away on a side road and the girl is the only person of her age in the whole area. She walked out with me to the road down a trail through the field in the deep snow. When I went to start Gabriel the battery was completely dead. It was about 35 below, so I wasn't surprised. While returning to the house the girl quite joyfully said,"Well, I guess there's nothing but for you to stay all night." But I had to get back to Burk's Falls that night. I called the garage and they came out and got the car started.
>
> The poor old lady got all worked up about me, for fear I wouldn't get the car going, so I went into her bedroom to explain that I was getting help from the garage and for her not to worry. To my surprise and

almost bewilderment, she reached up her two thin arms and putting a hand on my cheeks, drew me towards her and said, "I hope you get home alright, dearie. May God bless you and give you strength for your work, and I hope you'll say a little prayer for me sometimes."

I was fascinated by Doreen's stories and impressed by her dedication. By spring I felt that I had to share with Doreen my own deep affection. The opportunity came with the graduation banquet. We were invited to bring friends. I sent Doreen an invitation and she accepted. After the banquet, I took Doreen back to her sister Mary's home and there shared my love for her and asked her to be my partner for life. This was a very emotional time for both of us. It was as if a dam had burst and the pent up years of love had finally broken through. I realized that the hesitation had been all on my part. Doreen had been loving me all along. In a letter, after returning to Orville, she wrote:

> Oh Floyd, I do feel so happy - at times I think my heart must surely burst - it seems so overflowing with joy. Truly those two brief days we had together seem like a happy dream.

For me, expressing my feelings has been something I have had to learn all my life. No one has helped me to do this more than Doreen. In response to her letter I wrote: "I'm learning to love you more and more every day and it's the most exciting lesson I've ever attempted to learn."

In mid April I went to Orville for a few wonderful days with Doreen. In late May she got three weeks vacation and came to Toronto for my graduation. We spent some time with my parents and with hers. At the time of the ordination I learned that I had been appointed to the Esterhazy Pastoral Charge in Saskatchewan starting July 1st. Doreen had decided that she needed to remain on the Orville Pastoral Charge until the end of October, so we fixed on November 13th, 1948 for our wedding.

As November approached I made preparations for my return from Saskatchewan to Ontario for our wedding. Doreen left Orville in October and was making all the local arrangements in Lindsay. My plans were to leave by train on Monday morning after my week-end services, to arrive in Toronto by Wednesday and complete the arrangements. Monday morning I learned that Vernon Flook, the Postmaster and long-time elder, had died suddenly. I felt I couldn't leave before the funeral, which we arranged for Wednesday morning, so that I could catch the afternoon train to get me to Toronto by Friday. I wired Doreen asking her to get the marriage license and telling her that I would be there in time for the rehearsal Friday night. Little did I know the local Lindsay registrar would not issue a license unless both parties were present three days in advance. Fortunately, Doreen's father had a registrar friend in Oakwood who was not so particular and who agreed to issue a license which I could sign later.

The wedding took place in Doreen's home church, Queen St. United Church, Lindsay on Saturday. The only mishap was at the reception in the Agnew residence when the bridal veil caught fire from candles as Doreen and I cut the wedding cake. However, I saved the day by snatching off the veil with only a slight burn to my hand.

LIFE IN ESTERHAZY

Doreen quickly won the hearts of the people on the whole Esterhazy pastoral charge. The Lee family in Hazelcliffe had a special place in our hearts. Grandma Lee, a dear old Scottish lady, called us her "bairns." The youngest of the Lee sisters, Jean, became almost like a sister for Doreen. One weekend when I had to be away, Doreen agreed to take the church services in the three churches. She asked Jean to spend the weekend with her and accompany her on Sunday. Since the manse had no bathroom we had to take "sponge baths" in front of the kitchen stove. On Sunday morning, when Jean was bathing, suddenly she heard the back porch door open next to the kitchen. Jean panicked and fled to the next room. Doreen, who was upstairs, saw Jean's nude figure at the bottom of the stairs trying to escape from the "intruder." The intruder turned out to be Mrs. Bankey, our good friend and neighbour.

The three years Doreen and I spent in Esterhazy with loving friends were an ideal preparation for our later work together in Nayoro, Hokkaido. We also felt supported by the congregations we had served together. We kept in touch with many of them and always made a point of visiting them whenever we returned to Canada.

MINISTRIES OF LOVE IN HOKKAIDO

Life for Doreen in Nayoro was not easy. For one thing communicating in Japanese was always a struggle. Both of us took two years of language study in Tokyo. The first year Doreen accompanied me to the Naganuma Japanese Language School, but after Dennis was born in August of our second year, Doreen stayed home and studied with a tutor and was not able to devote full time to language study. In a talk she gave at Covenant College in March of 1969 she said:

> Whatever I have been able to do has been limited by two factors. First and foremost has been trying to communicate in a language that gets the reputation of being one of the most difficult in the world to read and write and speak. Ordinary conversation has become possible, but religious discussions, speeches or sermons, radio and T.V. programs often have spots in them that leave me to my imagination, with the result that one feels a bit stupid most of the time.

> Another factor that has limited the scope of missionary work for me has been teaching our three children by the Ontario Department of Education Correspondence Course. Of course they attended Japanese school too, but after returning home each day they had to pursue their studies in English.

In spite of her lack of facility in the language, it did not prevent her from making some of the deepest friendships with many Japanese women, who responded to her love with heartfelt affection. Japanese women tend to be very formal and polite and it is often difficult to break through their reserve. However, it was not long before Doreen had developed intimate friendships with a wide variety of women in Nayoro. These included neighbourhood cooking classes, the Women's Group in the church, a weekly Bible study group in our home, flower arranging groups, a women's English class, and a community art class.

It also wasn't long before she was asked to teach western cooking in our home. Once a week neighbourhood women would crowd into our kitchen to learn how to cook simple wholesome meals. For instance, we had found that liver was the cheapest meat that we could buy since most people did not eat liver. What better way was there to economize than to learn to eat liver? So she taught them how to cook a liver dish, without telling them first what it was. They were surprised but enjoyed the meal. After that we found that more and more people in the town started buying liver and the price went up.

The church Women's Group met monthly and discussed various topics having to do with faith and social issues. For one of the meetings she was asked to give a talk on "sex tours" by Japanese men to East Asian countries. The women of the United Church of Christ in Japan had taken this up as an issue, and had carried out demonstrations at stations in Tokyo against men departing on "sex tours." This talk prompted one of the liveliest discussion they ever had in that group.

Doreen was also asked to preach a few sermons both in Nayoro and the outlying church groups. Her main tasks in the church, however, was playing the organ for church services, weddings and funerals, in visitation and in hosting people in our home. Guests were always interested in our child-rearing customs. For instance, most Japanese mothers with fussy babies or children would try to silence them by putting caramel candies in their mouths. We soon let it be known that we did not feed our children sweets and did not want them being fed candies. Because we often had evening guests in our home we set strict bed-time guide lines for the children. The children could come down and meet the guests but then were expected to soon after settle down and go to sleep. The guests were surprised that most times we were successful.

HOME VISITATION - JAPAN STYLE

Doreen soon became involved in a home visitation programme of the church women's group. She describes one of these visits:

> One day I did some home visitation on behalf of the women's group of the Nayoro church. I accompanied a young mother with her two children. We had to drive several kilometres into the country to visit the first home - a dilapidated farm home where the mother is a Christian. As we made our way up the long path from the roadway we debated as to where to try to enter. Stepping over broken floorboards we entered the outside entranceway, scaring the chickens out of the way. At this point the woman appeared from the room on the right. She seemed embarrassed to have guests - especially when one was a foreign person. In fact she did not even invite us in, which is very unusual for a Japanese person - but rather apologized for the state of things. Her husband had been in the hospital for some time and that week a sore hand had prevented her from doing anything.
>
> The whole place was a picture of dejection and the same feeling was mirrored in the eyes of the woman as she spoke to us. We assured her of the interest of the church women and gave her a church periodical to read and went on our way.
>
> Several weeks later when Floyd went to the evening service, arriving early he noticed a woman sitting near the back. She was the same woman I had visited. She explained that she had been in town to visit her husband in the hospital and before going home she had come to the church to pray. She could not

wait for the evening service since she had to get back home, so Floyd and one of the church elders who had arrived by this time prayed for her. Who knows, perhaps our visit had reminded her of God's concern and love for her, drawing her to God's house to pray.

BIBLE STUDY GROUP

Shortly after we arrived in Nayoro we formed a weekly, Wednesday morning Bible study group in our home, especially for women who did not go to church but were interested in the study of the Bible. Four of our neighbours attended and became close friends, Mrs. Reiko Fujiwara, Mrs. Tsuta Gonoji, Mrs. Noriko Kihara, and Mrs. Ryoko Nagaoka. Ordinarily Japanese seldom use "given names" except within the family or with the closest of friends. Before long, however, they were calling her Doreen San, a term of affection, rather than the more formal Howlett Sensei - teacher Howlett.

Although these four neighbours never joined the church, they remained faithful members of the Bible study group for over twenty years. The Bible came to mean a great deal to their lives and this showed up in the way they lived and the service projects they undertook. As one means of living out their faith and serving the community the four of them took on a project of going to the town library once a week to record tapes for the blind. This service continued for many years. We gave them the nickname of "the four troubadours" since they did so many things together.

Doreen describes a visit by the Bible study group to a mother and her disabled son in an isolated area in the country:

> The group of neighbourhood women who have been studying the Bible in our home had a new experience this November. During the summer and fall they had been knitting blocks to make a woollen afghan for a handicapped boy, Miyaou Usui. When the afghan was completed, we drove some 30 kilometres to an isolated farm home, where Miyaou, now in his early

twenties, lives. Ever since his early childhood he has been confined to his futon (padded quilt) lying on the floor - not even able to sit up or feed himself. All these years his mother has cheerfully and lovingly cared for him, often by herself, since his father's work as a woodsman takes him away from home for long periods of time.

For the past few years she has been reading the Bible to him as together they had enrolled in a Bible radio correspondence course. Two years ago, as a result of that course he had asked to be baptized, and a year later his mother also received baptism. The day we visited them, taking the afghan, was a happy occasion for all. Miyaou was so delighted with the brightly coloured afghan that he rolled around on his quilt, smiling and saying "thank you" in his halting speech. His mother was especially happy to have women her own age to chat with. She confided something of her years of hardship with seeing her son crippled with polio as a baby. But through it all she had maintained a cheerful disposition - and this with her faith in God for strength to face each day - made a real impression on the Nayoro women, and, in turn, strengthened their faith.

Mrs. Chieko Tsuji, the wife of a local druggist, was another person with whom Doreen developed a meaningful friendship. One day when Doreen was in the drug store Mrs. Tsuji mentioned that she had heard there was a Bible study group in our home and would like to join. Mrs. Tsuji's first husband had died when she was young and she was then married by her family to an autocratic Japanese man much older than herself.
    Although she knew her husband would be opposed to her studying Christianity she said that since she had just turned fifty she thought she was able to make up her own mind. It happened that at that time Doreen was also fifty so this made another bond between them. Mrs. Tsuji started to attend the

group and for the first few times after about an hour there would be a phone call from her husband, saying the store was getting very busy, could she come home right away. She didn't pay any attention and would remain to the end. Finally, the husband gave up calling. Mrs. Tsuji and Doreen had many long talks about how to deal with the stresses of home life, and after a time the husband grudgingly admitted that she had changed and he became easier to live with.

ART CLASS

Mrs. Tsuji had always wanted to study art. There was an excellent art teacher, Masayoshi Nakaya, who taught art to a group that met weekly. Mrs. Tsuji urged Doreen to join the art class with her. Doreen said she didn't think she had any talent, since she had never enjoyed art in high school taught by a teacher without any creativity. However, she soon became completely engrossed in oil painting. It was a new hobby which gave her enormous satisfaction. She discovered that she did have a talent and produced some beautiful works of art. Before we left Japan the other art students urged her to put on an art show. She agreed to do this if the others would also display their works along with hers. Many people from the town and even from as far away as Sapporo came to the show.

Another bonus of joining the art class was that it opened her up to an entirely new circle of friends. One former acquaintance who became a close friend was Mrs. Tomiko Kawakami. Mrs. Kawakami's husband Nobuo was a professor at the Nayoro women's college, and they lived near our home. Their daughter and our daughter, Susan, were the same age and went to the church kindergarten and Japanese elementary school together. The Kawakamis had always participated in annual peace events organized by the church, were ardent peace activists and were leaders in the local Communist Party. Tomiko was one of the leaders of the art group and an excellent artist herself. Doreen found that not only were they bound together by a mutual love for art, but they shared a vision for a peaceful world and a more just society.

THE KAWAKAMIS STORY

I don't think Doreen ever heard the story about how Tomiko and Nobuo got together and their reason for their peace activism. As a young student, Nobuo had been an ardent nationalist. He had joined the Japanese navy and had volunteered to be a "kamikaze" suicide bomber. They were trained to man under-water torpedoes to blow up battleships. Fortunately, the war ended before he was able to carry out his mission. With the Japanese defeat he fell into a deep despondency. It was Tomiko who helped him turn his life around. Her experience of the war had been completely different. She was a teacher living in Tokyo. Four times her home was bombed, but she could not leave Tokyo because her family was dependent on the income from her teaching job. She helped Nobuo see how he had been brainwashed into becoming part of the war machine, and because of the horror of the atomic bombing they decided to devote their lives to working for peace. At that time the best instrument for working for peace seemed to be the Communist Party, which in Japan was taking a lead in peace activities. Doreen and I both had a great deal of respect for the Kawakamis and treasured their friendship.

IKEBANA

Doreen loved Japanese "ikebana" flower arranging. She had started taking ikebana lessons while still in Tokyo. When we came to Nayoro she was introduced to Mrs. Hiroe Miura, a gracious woman, accomplished in the traditional Japanese arts of tea ceremony and ikebana. Since some of Doreen's neighbours and friends were also interested in studying ikebana she invited Mrs. Miura to hold weekly lessons in our home. Mrs. Miura brought flowers for each of the women to create an arrangement following certain rules, but also using their own imaginations. After the arrangements were finished they sat down to admire each others creations, to drink tea and talk. This became a weekly event which was a highlight in all their lives.

Mrs. Miura became one of Doreen's close friends and started coming to the weekly Bible study. After a few years, when her husband retired, they moved to Chiba, near Tokyo.

She kept up her interest in the Bible, lived out many of the Christian virtues but never did become a baptized Christian. To us making a formal connection with the church was never the most important thing. Since her new home was close to the Narita airport, whenever we returned to Canada she insisted on coming to the airport to see us off and giving us a parting gift.

ENGLISH CONVERSATION CLASSES

Doreen also did some part time teaching of English conversation at the Dohoku Centre English School. A group of prominent women of the town asked her to be their teacher. This group included, the wife of a dentist, Dr. Gama, the chair of the Nayoro/Lindsay Twinning Committee, a doctor's wife, the wife of a cake shop owner, the wife of a large electrical shop, the owner and hostess of a night-club restaurant, and the wife of an engineer. This group never became very proficient in English but they did have a good time together and appreciated Doreen's friendship. For recreation they invited Doreen to go with them to the local hot-springs hotel where they could get into the pool together and enjoy some "skinship."

SUPPORT FOR PASTOR'S WIVES

Doreen was also a source of strength to the wives of the pastors in the northern region. All of them had come from main island of Honshu, far from their homes and were often very lonely. Doreen tells of a two-day retreat for pastor's wives:

> It was the first time a retreat for pastor's wives was held in this area. It had the whole-hearted co-operation of their husbands who looked after the children to let the mothers attend. We held the retreat in our home, starting at lunch on one day and finishing the following day in mid afternoon. My impression was that these women were starved for this kind of fellowship. They talked together so steadily that it was hard to get them to break off to eat their meals. We all felt convinced that we should do this each year

and the ministers went so far as to write it in their schedules for the coming year.

The wives' retreat became a tradition for the following years. This meant that Doreen kept alive close connections with the wives of the pastors.

MINISTRIES TO THE MENTALLY ILL

Among those most appreciative of Doreen's caring love were patients suffering from mental illness in the local hospital. Dr. Kumagai, the hospital psychiatrist was a dedicated Christian and a member of the Nayoro church. He encouraged any of his patients that were well enough to leave the hospital to attend the Nayoro church service on Sunday mornings. Often four or five of the patients would take advantage of this opportunity. Doreen frequently invited them home for lunch. In our home, they enjoyed listening to good music and joining in conversation in a freer atmosphere than they had in the hospital.

One of the most frequent Sunday visitors was Shinya Kageyama. Over the years Doreen and I became like parents to him. My first contact with Shinya was when Mitsuko Hosoumi, the minister of the Shibetsu church asked me to accompany her to the Shibetsu hospital to see a man who had attempted to end his life by taking poison. He had been discovered in time and his life was saved, but with some crippling effects to his body. He had attended Shibetsu High School and had been able to pass the stiff examinations to get into medical school at Hokkaido University. However, as frequently happens to those who go through the "examination hell" to get into a good university, he developed a mental illness during his first year and was forced to drop out. He got a job with a construction gang, always hoping to get back into university. When he finally discovered that it would not be possible to return he became very despondent and attempted suicide. During his high school days he had attended church "house meetings" in Shibetsu and also had as a mentor in university a Christian professor whom he greatly admired. He told us later that the visit from Mitsuko

Hosoumi and myself in his hospital room was as if Jesus had come to visit. The visit gave him new hope.

On release from the hospital he attended church and was baptized. However, while working with the construction gang he had developed an addiction to alcohol and sometimes when he became despondent he drank. One day he got drunk, fell down stairs and hit his head. He was unconscious for a week, but it so happened that one of the students who had started with him in medicine at Hokkaido University was now a brain surgeon. This doctor operated on him and saved his life. As soon as he was discharged, he boarded a train to come back to Nayoro to see us. He spent several nights with us until we got him into the Nayoro hospital under Dr. Kumagai's care. Since that time he has led a fairly stable life. After leaving the hospital he got a job as a parking lot attendant and made frequent visits to our home. When he heard we were returning to Canada he was devastated for a time. Doreen's death in 1992 was another big shock to him. He misses Doreen very much. From time to time he phones me from Japan and a conversation cheers him up. He is still like a son to me.

Doreen was able to enter into many circles of town life and develop close friendships with a wide variety of people. Later, when it came time for us to go back to Canada, many of these friends came to say goodbye with tears in their eyes. Doreen had been able to make a deep and lasting impact on many people in Nayoro.

MUSIC LEADERSHIP

One of the activities that Doreen missed most in coming to Japan was not being able to pursue her interest in playing the pipe organ. There were no pipe organs in Hokkaido and only old pump organs in the churches in the north. However, she did have many requests to play pump organs in the churches and she frequently played the organ for Sunday service in the Nayoro church. She was also called upon to play for weddings and funerals, not only in Nayoro but also in many other communities. Few of the churches had choirs, but each Christmas she would get together a small choir to sing Christmas carols.

ENCOUNTER WITH ILLNESS

Doreen's health had been good until the winter of 1974 when she had to go to Tokyo for the removal of kidney stones. The doctor ended up taking away one third of one kidney. Recovery was slow, but Doreen said that although being sick is not pleasant, it has its compensations. One of these was finding out just how many friends she had. Besides many letters from friends both in Japan and Canada, she was visited almost every day while in the hospital by Tokyo friends.

Her illness also drew together the women in the Bible study group during her absence. During her absence many of the women joined in spoken prayer for the first time, praying earnestly for Doreen's full recovery. After her return home they were very helpful, coming in frequently to assist with the housework and bringing gifts of food.

FAMILY LIFE

Creating a happy and wholesome family life was very important to Doreen. She saw to it that in spite of our busy schedules we had time for the children. Dennis, Peter and Susan attended Japanese elementary school, but we also arranged that they take Ontario Correspondence Courses in English. The main burden for teaching fell on Doreen. The "English school time" took place both before and after Japanese school. The children would complain that their Japanese friends didn't have to study that much, but they became completely bilingual. When we returned to Canada for our home assignment years they had no difficulty fitting into Canadian schools.

After our second Canadian home assignment we took back a family-sized tent so that we could camp in the summer vacation period. Unfortunately our camping trips were all too brief. Japanese schools only had one month of vacation in the summer and part of this was taken up with English Camps for Japanese junior and senior high school students. However, each summer we did manage to get away for short camping trips to some of Hokkaido's many beauty spots like Lake Doya and Lake Shikotsu in the south and the Akan national park in the southeast.

We have many happy memories of exploring the caves at Nakatombetsu with Gordon Morwood and climbing to the top of Mount Rishiri Fuji on Rishiri island off the northeast coast of Hokkaido. Every spring the whole family travelled to Honshu by train and ferry for the annual "Kyodan Related Missionary Conference" usually held at hot-spring resorts in Hakone. This was a chance to get together with other missionary families from Canada and the U.S. The autumn that the World Exposition was held in Osaka we drove down through the spectacular scenery of the west coast Japan Sea area. We returned by way of Tokyo where we left Peter and Dennis who were then attending the American School in Japan.

By the beginning of 1981 we both felt it was time to leave. Doreen had not fully recovered from her kidney operation, and we both wanted to have the experience of living and working in Canada again. We also felt that the work in Nayoro would not suffer with our departure. Rob and Keiko Witmer had come back to Nayoro and were happy to take over the work. Rob had an excellent facility with the Japanese language and Keiko who had grown up in Hokkaido had a good understanding of the society. They made an excellent team.

Packing up after so many years in one place was not easy. There were many interruptions as friends came to say goodbye. If we had not had Peter, who had just returned from Canada to live in Japan, to continue the packing while we visited with guests, we might never had got away from Nayoro. Leaving so many good friends in Nayoro and all of Northern Japan was a heart-rending experience. It was also sad parting with Peter, who had decided that he wanted to make his life's work in Japan, but there was the consolation that we also were leaving a part of ourselves in Japan, and knew that with him there we would return.

THE PRAIRIE CHRISTIAN TRAINING CENTRE
After our return to Toronto we had one year of sabbatical in which to have some rest and to travel among Canadian churches telling our Japan story. During the time in Toronto we began to look at future work in Canada. Because of our

experience with community and lay education work in Japan, I was most interested in the work of the lay training centres in Canada. In May of 1982 I got word that the Prairie Christian Training Centre (P.C.T.C.) in Fort Qu'Appelle, Saskatchewan was looking for a staff person. I immediately sent an inquiry letter to P.C.T.C. The Rev. Walter Farquharson, Chair of the Board, invited me to fly out for their upcoming Board meeting for an interview, at which I was accepted as part of the Staff Team. The team consisted of three Programme Staff, two Office Secretaries, two Maintenance Personnel, and the Kitchen Supervisor. I was delighted to become one of the Programme Staff and to be a part of a total staff team that had no one person as "director" but democratically worked together to carry out the programme of the Centre.

For Doreen and myself there could have been no better appointment. It was good to be back in Saskatchewan where we had many good friends. Living at P.C.T.C. meant that we immediately became a part of the loving and progressive community and took part in the wide variety of Centre programmes. Doreen was particularly happy to participate in music events with hymn writers Jim and Jean Strathdee and Jim Manley. We lived in a staff house overlooking beautiful Echo Lake in the scenic Qu'Appelle Valley. Doreen also had the opportunity of assisting in the programmes of the Centre. We had six very happy years at P.C.T.C., from 1982 to 1988.

MINISTRY IN THE PHEASANT CREEK PASTORAL CHARGE

In 1986 Doreen was invited to join the Pheasant Creek Pastoral Charge Parish Team as a part-time minister. The Pheasant Creek Pastoral charge was made up of four churches; Balcarres, Abernethy, Lemberg and Duff. Doreen's responsibilities included taking church services at two of the churches twice a month and visitation throughout the parish. She really appreciated using skills which she did not have the opportunity to fully utilize in Japan. In sermons she spoke out strongly on social issues. Shortly before she was to leave, a farmer, who had the reputation of being somewhat macho, said to her "You sometimes made me mad, but I respect you for what you said. You gave me a lot to think about."

In a sermon she preached at the Balcarrres church on April 17th, 1988 on the "Ecumenical Decade for the Churches in Solidarity with Women" she said:

> My own journey - or conscientization - has been going on for some years now. I can recall when the feminist movement came to the fore that I brushed it aside and thought it wasn't a concern of mine to worry about. I was happily married, fulfilled in affairs of my family and church, living in Japan where it certainly had not become an issue. Then on a home assignment here in Canada I became aware of the language issue. Up until then the hymns hadn't bothered me as being male oriented. Even at that time I thought too big a fuss was being made. But when my daughter refused to sing many hymns with me at the piano - even disliked going to church because of the male dominated services and hymns, I began to see sexist language through her eyes and couldn't remain indifferent any longer. I give her credit for a lot of my growth, but I have to admit that I still have a long way to go.

Doreen also enjoyed visitation of the older people in the parish. I remember going with her for a lunch with Elsa Webster, an eighty-year-old who lived in a large farmhouse by herself. She urged Doreen to drop in at any time for a rest when she was out visiting. Another eighty-year old who lived in the village of Balcarres knit her a large many-coloured afghan to show Doreen her appreciation.

RETIREMENT TO ONTARIO

In 1988 we decided to leave Saskatchewan and retire in Ontario, where Dennis and Susan and their families were living. I had already extended two years beyond the usual 65 year retirement age. It was again hard to pull up stakes and leave another community and the friends we had made there. Since we did not know where we wanted to live, we found rented rooms in Toronto to give us time to look around. From September to December I took a part time job as Co-director of the Ecumenical Forum for Global Ministries, the inter-church agency which does training for overseas missionary personnel.

In August we rented a cottage on Sturgeon Lake, near Lindsay, and started looking for a suitable place in which to retire, in the region of Peterborough. In our travels we saw the sign to Lakefield, and said, "Let's take a look, if it was good enough for Margaret Lawrence, our favourite novelist, maybe it will be right for us." Driving through the Lakefield downtown, a "For Sale" sign at a red brick bungalow on Prospect St. caught our eye. We arranged to look at that house and several others the next week. We ended up buying that first house we had seen and found it just right for us. We moved there in January of 1989.

With some help from my brother Ralph, who had house-building skills, we built three rooms and a toilet in the basement so that we had accommodation for family and friends when they came to visit. There was a large garden space with a big raspberry patch. We enjoyed furnishing the first home of our own and soon made friends in the community. Before long we joined the Kawartha Ploughshares peace group and found a new circle of friends in Peterborough. We helped to found the Friends of Affirm group in support of gay and lesbian people. It wasn't long before both Doreen and I were getting invitations to speak at churches and women's groups in the region. In the winter we skied across the fields near our home. These were really happy years for us.

HEALTH PROBLEMS CAST A SHADOW

The years together in "retirement" in Lakefield were all too brief. Shortly after going to Lakefield we found a compassionate family doctor, Doctor Leger, who on doing a medical examination discovered that Doreen had a distinct heart murmur. Dr. Leger sent Doreen to a heart specialist in Peterborough who gave her extensive tests and told us we must monitor her heart function carefully. In the winter of 1992 she felt more fatigued.

She went to the specialist again and he sent her for an angiogram in Toronto. However, it took a month before we could get the appointment. The angiogram disclosed the need for an urgent heart valve replacement. Although we had apprehension about a major heart operation, we knew a number of people who had new valves and returned to good health. Getting an appointment to see a surgeon took another month. Before we were able to get to see the surgeon, Doreen had a sudden heart attack and died.

The evening before she died, she and I attended the opening service for the Bay of Quinte Conference Annual Meeting of the United Church that was held in Peterborough that year. The evening worship was a meaningful communion service with music by Jim and Jean Strathdee, our favourite hymn writers, whom we had known at music events at PCTC. It was a deeply emotional time for both of us to join in singing with them and to take part in a communion service in which Jim and Jean also gave leadership.

The next morning, I was planning to attend the conference but Doreen was staying home. Just as we were about to eat breakfast, Doreen said, "There's something wrong" and clutched her heart. She asked me to call Jean Jackman, a retired nurse who lived two doors from us. However, by the time Jean got there Doreen had died of a heart attack. I phoned Dennis and Susan in Toronto who came immediately and also phoned Peter in Japan. He said that he and the family would fly over in time for the memorial service. The service was held with the whole family and a large number of friends present giving us their support. We asked the Rev. Alan McLean, who had lived with us for three years in Japan, to give the memorial sermon. Here are a few words from his tribute:

> To me Doreen embodied so many of the best aspects of the United Church Tradition. A deep, quiet faith which always had reference to the world with its pains and its joys. As Doreen learned about a new issue, or need, or a matter of simple justice or human decency, she would take up the cause as well as she

could, for she could do nothing else. Her faith would not allow her to turn away.

Alan's words brought comfort to me and thankfulness for the life that Doreen and I had shared together.

LIVING WITH GRIEF

I was devastated by the sudden loss of my life's companion. Susan stayed with me for a week to give support, but after that I was on my own. For a long time it seemed so unreal. I regretted that, even though we knew her condition was serious, I never really talked with Doreen about the possibility of her death.

Several months after her death I was asked to take the three services on the Apsley pastoral charge. I decided to share some of my sorrow and struggle with the congregations. They knew Doreen, since she had also led worship in these churches previously. I will quote a few portions of my sermon:

> As many of you know my wife Doreen died suddenly on May 29th. It was a great shock to me and to many of her friends. Since then as I have struggled with my loss and loneliness, I have thought more deeply on the meaning of life and the meaning of death.
>
> I can see now that for me the challenge is not to spend my days pitying myself over my loss, but rather seeing how I can grow through this period of grief. How can I use this experience of loss in becoming more sympathetic towards others facing similar experiences? How can I become more aware of hurting people all around me and in the world as a whole?
>
> As I reflect on the ways I can grow as I seek to honour the memory of Doreen I see that I am called to make a renewed effort in all these areas of concern which were so dear to Doreen's heart. I need to see how

all these causes of liberation and justice can become more integrated into my faith and action in the days ahead.

I am writing this ten years after Doreen's death. I still miss her greatly, but I find meaning in life by continuing to immerse myself in the causes on which we formerly worked at together - issues of peace, justice, equality and democratic government. I am blessed that in Sheila Nabigon-Howlett, I have found a loving partner and a wife, whom Doreen and I both came to know in the Kawartha Ploughshares peace group, a woman who shares the same passion for peace, justice and faith-based living.

Doreen's ikebana lesson with neighbour women and Susan

9

FAMILY REFLECTIONS

Susan, the youngest in our family, has worked in a Hosiery Mill in Toronto as a knitting machine operator and was active in the union health and safety committee. She next worked as a community legal worker advocating for people seeking workers' compensation. She then went on to train to become a midwife and is now working with three other midwives in Peterborough and the surrounding area. She finds a great satisfaction in her new vocation. She and her partner Bruce McFarlane live in Lakefield with their two daughters, Hanah and Naomi. The whole family loves camping, gardening, and music.

Dad asked me to write about my experience and perspective of growing up in Japan. It's difficult to put the experience into a nutshell, but I'll focus on the Nayoro childhood years. My grandma, Hilda Howlett, spent a year and a half in Nayoro before I was born. She came to help around the time of my brother Peter's birth. I found it fascinating to read the journal she kept during that time. I was able to get a daily glimpse of the life of the family I was about to enter into. Dennis was a lively, talkative toddler at that time and he filled Grandma's journal with many endearing moments. Life in the Howlett home was bustling. Grandma pitched in with the chores with good old-fashioned pioneer vigor. What she accomplished in a day I'd be proud to do in a month! I know I come from good strong stock!

I was the youngest of Floyd and Doreen's three children. With two boys, they were really hoping for a girl, so I'm glad that I fulfilled their hopes! I was "made in Japan," but born in Canada on my family's one-year home assignment. We returned to Japan when I was six months old, so my first memories are of Japan.

We were the only "gaijin" (foreigner) family in town, so we grew up immersed in the Japanese neighbourhood. Inside our home, we lived as a Canadian family, but once we stepped outside, we spoke Japanese and felt very much a part of the fabric of life that surrounded us. I think due to the fact that we were children, our neighbours let their guard down more often and we were able to get more candid glimpses of their lives than my parents. Our neighbours were curious about our lives too, and asked many questions about our family.

We lived in a western-style house that was built the year my parents moved to Nayoro. We spent may hours playing in the yard, riding our tricycles and pulling the wagon along the sidewalk, playing on the swings beside the house, and in the winter, building snow forts with the plentiful snow. Dad always planted a big vegetable garden in the spring. Mom was busy in the summer harvesting the produce and during the early years making preserves and canning, and in the later years, freezing them for winter food. Mom also tended a beautiful flowerbed behind the house and beside the front door. As a young child I loved to smell the flowers and was fascinated by the white, yellow and monarch butterflies that fluttered about the flowers. We spent many hours in the raspberry patch picking berries during the summer holidays.

Our house was always open to visitors. Neighbours without a telephone used to come over to use ours. We kids in turn, went to our neighbours' houses to watch television as we didn't get a television set until I was about ten years old! Couples would come for counseling, there were Bible study and English study groups, and ex-psychiatric patients found refuge in our home where they felt accepted for who they were. Even with her faltering Japanese, my mother's warmth and kindness were clearly evident to all she befriended.

I spent many hours visiting the grandmothers and aunties on our street. One of my very favorite grandmothers was "Maeda-san" who lived two doors away. She lived in a household with an extended family spanning four generations. Unlike many post-war women of her age who adopted western clothing, Mrs. Maeda continued to wear the kimono throughout her life. We were kindred spirits. I used to love to sit on the tatami (straw mat floor) at a low table, sipping Japanese tea and eating her home-made "okoko" (pickled daikon radish) or my favorite rice crackers. We spent hours talking. She seemed to be amused seeing the world through my eyes, and I loved her attention. I was fascinated by the everyday activities in this household, which were very different from ours. Maeda-san was the 'younger' grandmother in this family. Her mother was an ancient woman who used to sit by the stove all day, with a rounded back. There was always something cooking on the stove and they would often give me a sample. The older grandmother would sometimes let me sit quietly beside her in front of their Buddhist altar in the back room while she lit the incense, made her offerings, and said her prayers. She would let me ring the bell after her prayer was finished. Maeda-san's husband spent his spare time pruning his many bonsai trees along the windowsill. In the early evening the whole family would gather around the television set to watch sumo wrestling.

After I returned to Canada, I kept having dreams about going back to see Maeda-san. I wanted her to meet my daughters. However, she passed away before I made it back to Nayoro with them. When I visited her daughter Fujiwara-san, she told me that old Mrs. Maeda had also been having dreams about me. I think we never stopped visiting each other.

During the earlier years Dad was away a lot, traveling to the surrounding communities by train and Jeep, and in the later years by station wagon. Sometimes we went along on trips and would be covered with a layer of dust from traveling on the winding dirt roads. When he got back, he always set aside time for "family night" when we'd sit in front of the fireplace and play games. Our favorite was "ghost in the graveyard." Mom often played the piano and we'd sing together. Once the Dohoku Christian Center was established, he was around more often. As we got older, we participated in some of the activities there. When we were in high school we helped to teach English at the English camps and made some good friends; with some of whom we still keep in touch. Some of my best memories were our family camping trips. Every summer, we went for a trip to a different part of Hokkaido. This was long before campgrounds were established so we would just find a spot beside a lake, the sea, or deep in the mountains, beside a river.

World issues were often discussed around the dinner table. I used to listen keenly to Dad's interpretation of world events. I learned to respect his insights and analysis, although I didn't have words for that when I was little. Dad instilled in us a strong sense of social justice and the importance of continuing to learn throughout life, always with a critical mind. From Mom, I learned about the gentle, yet profound ways of relating to the world around us. She used to have a "quiet time" each morning when she retreated to her bedroom, read and contemplated before getting caught up in the hustle and bustle of life. She emanated an inner peace and grace. She taught me the strength of compassion.

We went to the Nayoro church kindergarten and I became fluent in Japanese. However, when we returned to Canada for a year when I was six, I forgot most of the language. When we returned to Japan and I was placed in Japanese school, it took several months before I could speak again. I still remember the day when I was able to put up my hand for the first time and answer the teacher's question. She looked surprised to see my hand up. (The first Kanji character I read aloud was "foot.")

After school, we studied English simultaneously through a Canadian correspondence course, sent from Ontario. Mom was usually our teacher. It was difficult to keep up with both schools, so our correspondence courses fell behind. We had to catch up during the summer holidays. We weren't always the best pupils. When the doorbell would ring and Mom got busy with a houseguest, we'd be out the back door to play until she called us back. My favorite part about correspondence courses was reading about other children all around the world that were also taking the same correspondence course.

Being a "missionary kid" and a "preacher's kid" brought with it double expectations and assumptions about how we were to be. While in Japan, we were always reminded that we were very visible. When we came to Canada on home assignments, we were expected to perform at many of the church Sunday schools that my parents visited. When I was six, I used to dress in a kimono and do a dance I learned in Japanese kindergarten. I used to sing songs in Japanese with my brothers.

I used to cringe at the questions that always were asked based on Canadian stereotypes of the Japanese such as, "Do Japanese people live in paper houses?" I used to get frustrated because I had no way to articulate or describe my life in Japan.

Over the years, I saw how my parents' thinking evolved from starting at a place of essentially working to promote Christianity, to one of seeing it as their own spiritual roots but celebrating and respecting the human diversity in spirituality. Being immersed in another culture, the starting point for my understanding was that there are many different ways of expressing spirituality, and I have a deep respect for human diversity.

GROWING UP IN JAPAN: ACCORDING TO PETER

Peter studied Agriculture at the University of Guelph and worked in Canada for a few years before deciding he wanted to live in Japan. He is now living with his wife Suzuko and three children, Hanul, Kaya and Ellie in Nanae, a suburb of Hakodate, in the Southern tip of Hokkaido. He is teaching English at LaSalle High School and grows high bush blueberries on a one acre field. He is active in several environmental groups working on wind energy and energy conservation.

Growing up in a small town in Japan as the only "whites" was actually not such a different experience from growing up in any other situation. In the end, I think it is family relations which has the greatest influence on childhood development and in this regard I feel I have been very fortunate.

If I were to give one word to describe Dad, I would say he is "farmer." Growing up on a farm in West Montrose, Ontario he learned to work the land and care for farm animals from an early age. He learned that what was good for the land and all life and creatures living on it was good for all.

At our home in Nayoro, we had a large garden out back and many a summer morning I can remember waking up to the sound of the hoe scraping the earth. I would jump out of bed and look outside to find Dad in his ragged garden clothes and weathered leather garden shoes - weeding. The rhythm of his hoe was steady and he always had a determined look, knowing that he was doing the right thing.

We grew all types of vegetables; corn, carrots, radishes, potatoes, lettuce, broccoli, cauliflower, eggplants, beans, tomatoes, green peppers, parsnips, squash, pumpkins, and many more. Also, small fruits like raspberries, blackberries, black and red currents, gooseberries and rhubarb.

Dad taught me how first you must clean up the garden of last year's refuse and prepare the soil. He would gather all the corn stalks, the bean vines, the dried broccoli and cauliflower stalks and set them ablaze in the middle of the garden. I remember one year the refuse pile included branch trimmings and things and this pile got bigger and bigger. He set it ablaze one evening and on top of this fire with flames of three or so meters he threw on our dried out Christmas tree. The flames reached five to six meters now and that was enough for the fireman who kept watch from the fire tower in town to spot it. We heard the fire siren go and sure enough soon two red fire engines came screaming down the road followed by the multitudes of people who came out to "fire watch." Dennis, Susan and I were embarrassed and we hid in the raspberry patch and watched what was going to happen. However, nothing startled Dad and with his rake in hand he tended to the fire, making a simple apology when the fireman came, saying he would be careful next time.

To fertilize the garden every spring Dad would borrow the horse and cart of our neighbour, dairy farmer, Mr. Kurisu, and haul two or three cart-fulls of well decomposed manure. We would help him spread it so there was a thick dark blanket of manure over the whole garden. I remember once he was bitten by this horse because he had approached it from its blind eye side, but that didn't stop him from borrowing the same horse again the next year. Then after spreading two or three bagfulls of lime he would hire a local farmer to rotor-till the whole garden.

Next was the planting of the seeds - the dropping of these tiny specks of life into the hoed rows. I remember how Dad gave each of us kids a small space for our own gardens and we would plant all the veggies we liked best. Then next came the thinning. Now, let me say, Dad was no perfectionist gardener.

He was not one to have a straight-rowed no-weed garden. He never did like those tedious time consuming tasks. So, for his thinning of the lettuce and carrots he would simply use the one tip of his hoe and he'd whack out sections at set intervals and let what remained carry on.

Then comes weeding, oh weeding. This is the task I think Dad does best. He taught me that there is no end to this task. We pull out the bad and believe in the good. But he never used herbicides and he never aimed for a 100% kill. He'd pull out the worst to give the vegetables a chance and leave it at that. His practical, common-sense approach to this task has taught me much about what our outlook on life should be.

Then comes the harvest, the digging up of the root crops, the picking and gathering of the fruits and vegetables. Picking berries was a good time for talking and I can remember some good talks with Mom and Dad in the berry patch. And finally the eating of our produce. Dad always had a sense of thankfulness, but also a sense of receiving that which he deserved.

So, I learned much from Dad in the garden. But, I want to describe Dad as "farmer" not only because of what he taught me in the garden but because I can see that he has been a "farmer" in all his other activities. Watching him prepare his sermon with all kinds of books spread over his desk reminds me so much of the way he prepared the soil. Watching him at the small house church services and the Sanai (Three Love Schools) Farmers' Meetings reminds me so much of when he planted the seeds. And the writing of all those "letters to the editor" reminds me of his weeding. The removal or pointing out of the bad and injustices and praising the good. His approach to all he did was as a "farmer" and I thank him for this.

Memories of my childhood are filled with all those good times in nature. Wading in the river catching fish, tobogganing on the river bank, skating on the frozen river, picnics, family camping, cross country skiing, climbing trees visiting the Kurisu's dairy farm down the road, staring at the owl which happened to come by our local woods. And this deep bond with nature, formed during my childhood, is what moves me now to work to try to save this precious earth. For we humans face no greater task now than the recovery of mother nature, and the finding of the sacred balance we have lost.

GROWING UP IN JAPAN: ACCORDING TO DENNIS

While still studying at York University, Dennis began to work for GATT-Fly, a church related coalition dealing with societal issues in Canada and overseas. The name was later changed to the "Ecumenical Coalition for Economic Justice," a title that more closely described its function. From that he moved to the sister coalition of "Ten Days for Global Justice" as the National Coordinator. In 2001, when the coalitions were amalgamated into KAIROS: Canadian Ecumenical Justice Initiatives, Dennis became the Team Leader of the Canadian Justice Cluster, with responsibility for issues of poverty, health, refugees, the environment and aboriginal rights in Canada. He and his partner Elaine live with Daniel, Timothy, Brendan and David in Toronto.

From the time I was in junior high school, I was involved in Dohoku Centre programs. The leadership skills I gained and the educational philosophy and methodologies were very influential in my career direction.

A fundamental principle in all Centre programming was the respect for the participants' experience and knowledge and a commitment to creating a space where everyone was encouraged to participate and where everyone's contribution was valued. This was in strong contrast to the prevailing educational approach in Japan which was very hierarchical and content-oriented rather than experiential. Participants in Centre programs were often struck by the egalitarian and democratic atmosphere at the Centre.

Centre programs such as the Junior High and Senior High School English Camps incorporated these principles by seeking student input in program planning, giving ample time for participants to introduce themselves to each other, incorporating various group communication and "warm-up" games in the program and ensuring plenty of small group discussion. Small group discussion was stimulated by showing a movie or having a short presentation that raised issues, but subjects for discussion were always presented in an open ended way and never with "an answer" presumed by an "expert." Small group discussions were facilitated by a group leader who helped lead the discussion by posing key questions and ensuring that everyone had an opportunity to participate. Japanese students were so starved for opportunities to discuss issues of concern, it was never difficult to open up lively discussion.

The Junior High and High School English Camps were always the highlights of my summer. I was involved in planning, teaching conversational English classes in the morning, leading crafts or other interest activities in the afternoons and participating in the evening programs which featured discussion of social and educational issues of concern to students. I even learned how to play the guitar so that I could help to lead singing around the campfire. Camps were also places where close friendships were formed. One friend made at the English camps, Osamu Masaoka, was instrumental in arranging for me to go to Bangladesh in 1972 and later came to Canada to work with the Student Christian Movement at York University, which I helped to facilitate.

When I left Japan to attend York University I was introduced to the book *Pedagogy of the Oppressed* by Paulo Freire by one of my professors, Helene Mousa. I was so excited reading this powerful book, partly because it described and articulated a theory for many of the things that were practised in the Dohoku Centre programs. Because of the Dohoku Centre experience, Paulo Freire's writings were not just some difficult academic theory but something that I immediately understood. In the early 1970s I was fortunate to have the opportunity of meeting Paulo Freire when he visited Toronto and sharing with him the Ah-hah Seminar popular education methodology that I had developed based on his theories. His interest and encouragement inspired me to write the book, *Ah-hah! A New Approach to Popular Education*, describing this method and the experience of how this method had been used in Canada and around the world to help oppressed and marginalized groups do an analysis of their own situation and develop strategies for action.

My father believed that decisions about faith should be made freely by each individual and not be imposed on anyone.

Adult baptism was also the accepted means of membership in the Japanese Kyodan church. Dad was always very respectful of others' faith beliefs, including his children, and never pushed his own religion on anyone. Although we were dedicated when we were babies, we were not baptized. Reading and dramatizing Bible stories, family prayers, Christmas carol and hymn singing around the piano and attending church were all part of our family practice. My parents certainly shared their faith with their children but it was always clear that we each had to make up our own minds.

When I was in Junior High School I expressed an interest in being baptised. Dad suggested we read the biography of J.S. Woodsworth together and discuss it as part of my "Catechism." We also read a book on the Christian faith by Wilbar Howard. Martin Luther King, Albert Schweitzer, and Ghandi were also important heroes of my parents and books about them were also in our house. Dad had a study full of books that interested me. I remember reading books by Kagawa, Koyama, Bonhoeffer, Cox, and Yoder. The Nayoro church required that those seeking to be baptized write an essay on what their faith means to them and why they want to join the church. I had to articulate my faith and really think through what this decision meant in terms of life-long commitment. I was then interviewed by a group of elders and the Minister. At the baptism service itself, each person being baptized had to read out their personal statement of faith. It made baptism much more meaningful than the way it is commonly practised in the church in Canada where it is often just assumed as one of the rituals that is just a "given."

An important part of my participation in the Japanese church was involvement in the anti-war demonstrations and other social justice events. The Nayoro church co-sponsored Hiroshima and Nagasaki Day memorials along with the Socialist Party and Communist Party and labour unions. I came to feel that it was a natural and necessary part of living our faith, both personally and as a faith community.

I also often accompanied my father to house church meetings and found the informal worship and discussion of personal and social issues to be some of the most meaningful worship experiences I have ever had. After introductions and warm social conversation, some hymns were sung, some time was given for participants to share concerns or issues they would like to discuss, Bible study and discussion related to these issues would take place and the meeting would close with prayer in which everyone was free to articulate their own prayers and concerns. It was the opposite of rote, ritual, and religion unrelated to life and lived experience that characterizes so much of the worship in churches. And it had a profound impact on my ecclesiology.

I was very fortunate to have the opportunity to work with my father and observe him at work at the Dohoku Centre and in the church. It gave me a clear understanding and appreciation for what his work was. The "team work" with my father established at an early age has continued to this day as my father has become a very active local group member of the Ten Days for Global Justice program and Kairos while I have worked at the National Office, of these organizations. We continue to work on the same issues and campaigns.

Howlett family in 1968: Dennis, Susan, Floyd, Peter and Doreen

10

FAITH INSIGHTS

In a strange and wonderful way my faith pilgrimage has been much influenced by Dr. Toyohiko Kagawa, a person whom I had the opportunity of meeting only three times. I heard him when he spoke to students at our Japanese language school in Tokyo, when he gave an illustrated lecture to missionaries at a national conference, and again at the International Christian University where he spoke on the establishment of rural co-operatives in Japan. Kagawa was a diminutive person with poor eye-sight and thick glasses, but full of vitality. I was immediately impressed by his love and passion for people of all walks of life.

I have already spoken of Kagawa's life and the influence the examples of his involvement in so many areas of Japanese society had for our work in the Dohoku Centre and the Three Love Movement. I would like to expand further on his theological outlook and the influence it had on my own theological thought.

Kagawa's theology influenced me even before I went to Japan. I picked up two of his books in a second-hand book store during the time I was attending College. Much of what he had to say resonated with my own theological journey.

One attraction that Kagawa had for me was his advocacy of the way of non-violence and peace. In 1929 in his book, *Love the Law of Life*, he wrote about the way of non-violence:

> Jesus was charged with the mission of redeeming his attackers, just as God does. Even though men should put him to death, he believed that God was able to save. Hence, it was in the belief that for the possessor of truth death has no significance, that the principle of non-resistance had its origin.

His faith in Christian non-violence was sorely tested by the Japanese invasion of China and again with the attack on Pearl Harbour in 1943. In 1940 he had been arrested and charged with engaging in peace propaganda that was subversive of the interests of the state. In November of 1943 he was arrested in Tokyo and endured nine days of intense questioning late into the nights but was finally released on the condition he confine his activities to the church.

I was also attracted by the centrality of the gospel of love and the links he made to the social gospel. I had doubts similar to his about the value of "creedal Christianity" with its emphasis on the sinfulness of humankind in need of some kind of magical redemption. In his book, *Meditations on the Cross*, he says:

> Should we live the Christ-life in actual practice, or is it enough to subscribe to a doctrine? It is easy enough to stay in one's study, but to live with beggars, and to associate with day labourers, that is difficult.

I agreed with his extreme optimism regarding human nature and its ethical possibilities motivated by a self-giving love.

How do we assess Kagawa's theological thought? I found on going to Japan that most of the post-war Japanese theologians were much entranced by the theology of the eminent Swiss theologian, Karl Barth. Most Japanese theologians dismissed Kagawa for being too simplistic and "untheological." Personally I related much more to Kagawa's theology than I did to that of some of the ministers graduating from theological colleges who were preaching Barthian theology to uncomprehending congregations. In fact, Kagawa was more popular in church circles in North America than he was in his own nation of Japan.

What attracted me most to Kagawa was the practical nature of his theology. It was not based on creeds and dogma, but on a faith in the love that Jesus had exemplified, and which he called all those who follow to imitate. The love of God for all classes and conditions of people dominates all Kagawa's writings and his actions.

BACK IN CANADA

During our period of mission service in Japan from 1951 to 1981 we returned to Canada four times for year long visits. These were referred to at first as "furlough years," but later the terminology was changed to "home assignment," which was actually more accurate. We were not "on leave of absence" but had definite responsibilities during that time "at home." Part of the year we were expected to travel from church to church, in some designated area of Canada, to tell the mission story. The rest of the year we were given the opportunity to carry on study and research related to our particular work overseas. I found these periods of study of particular value to reflect on the task in Japan and to explore new areas of academic study.

During my 1956-57 home assignment as a part of my work towards a Bachelor of Divinity I wrote a thesis on "The Ministry of the Laity." During 1962-63 as a partial fulfilment for a Master of Theology degree, I produced a thesis on "The Contemporary Theology of the Church as Mission and Its Implication for the Church in Japan." For the 1968-69 period I participated in a "Canadian Urban Training Course" (CUT) which consisted of a sociological approach to inner city issues. The final home assignment in 1975-76 I did some guided reading on "Liberation Theologies" and also applied the CUT methodology to rural issues in Canada, relating it to the work I was doing with rural youth in Japan. Each of these studies expanded my horizons and were significant milestones in my faith journey.

THE MINISTRY OF THE LAITY

As I have indicated previously, even while I was serving as a minister in Esterhazy I had significant reservations about the nature of the special "ministerial order" and its relation to the "laity." These reservations were deepened as a result of working as an ordained minister in the United Church of Christ in Japan. It appeared that the Japanese church had simply adopted the western church view of a special ordained ministry and added to it Japanese traditional hierarchical and patriarchal structures. Dr. E. Stanley Jones, after travelling around churches in Japan, described the Japanese church as, "a pastor-ridden church" and its members as "the pastor's 'tea boys'." My experiences in Canada and in Japan prompted me to undertake the in-depth study of "The Ministry of the Laity."

In 1954, the Second Assembly of the World Council of Churches, in a report on the laity, stated:

> The growing emphasis in many parts of the world on the function of the laity . . . springs from the re-discovery of the true nature of the church as the 'people of God'. The word laity must not be understood in a merely negative way as meaning those church members who are not clergy.

This meant that my study had to include reference to the nature of the church and the role of clergy as well as that of the laity. I took as my Biblical starting point the words of 1 Peter 2:9 (NRSV): "You are a chosen race, a royal priesthood, a holy nation, God's own people, in order that you may proclaim the mighty acts of him, who called you out of darkness into his marvellous light."

I interpreted this passage to mean that the whole people of God, not just a special ministerial order, are chosen to make known God's works of healing, peace and justice. During the Reformation, both Martin Luther and John Calvin vehemently attacked the Roman Catholic division of the church into two orders: a clergy: "a hierarchy established by Divine law - with spiritual authority of government, teaching and worship" and "those over whom power is exercised, who are governed, taught and sanctified - the laity." Luther exclaims:

> Here, indeed, are the roots of that detestable tyranny of the clergy over the laity; trusting in the external anointing by which their hands are consecrated, in the tonsure and in vestments, they not only exalt themselves above lay Christians, who are only anointed by the Holy Spirit, but regard them as dogs and unworthy to be included with them in the church. . . Here Christian brotherhood has perished, here shepherds have been turned into wolves, ser-

vants into tyrants, churchmen into worse than worldlings.

Luther goes on to say that within the Christian church (ecclesia) every occupation can be a holy calling:

> A cobbler, a smith, a farmer, each has the work and office of his trade, and yet all are alike consecrated priests and bishops, and everyone by means of his own work or office must benefit and serve one another.

Luther adds that the only true mark of the ministry within the body of Christ is that of "being the servant of all." Although Luther greatly enhances the role of the laity he later introduces considerable ambivalence with respect to the right to preach the Word and administer the sacraments so that to all intents and purposes, the clergy alone are allowed these privileges and the laity are still denied them altogether.

John Calvin shows the same ambivalence. He speaks much of the "priesthood of all believers," and under the presbyterian system gave a more democratic role for lay elders in the governance of the church. However, in his determination that in the church everything must be done "decently and in order" he retained a unique role for the clergy. King James I is reported to have said, "The new presbyter is but old priest writ large."

The original insights of Luther and Calvin with regard to the status of every Christian in the church as the people of God were followed more closely by Menno Simons and the Anabaptists. Menno Simons, the father of the Mennonite tradition, declared:

> The true messengers of the Gospel who are one with Christ in spirit, love and life, teach that which is entrusted to them by Christ, namely repentance and the peaceable Gospel of grace which He Himself has received of the Father and taught the world.

It appears that the doctrines of ministerial order in the mainline churches tended to fall into the mould set by the Reformers, and to stifle a true theology of the laity. H.H. Walz, writing in the Ecumenical Review of the World Council of Churches, argues that actually there is a greater New Testament justification for the development of a theology of the laity than there is for a theology of the clergy. The term "laos" from which the word laity is derived occurs frequently in Biblical terminology where it refers to "the people." In the New Testament "laos" takes on the meaning of the "new people of God." The term "clergy" does not appear until much later in Christian literature when "clergy" and "laity" came to be regarded as two separate bodies, of which the "clergy" was superior.

MARTIN LUTHER KING JR.
Although not usually recognized as a black liberation theologian, Martin Luther King was a precursor of black liberation theology. King, who was elected President of the Southern Christian Leadership Conference, became the spokesman for a struggle which culminated in a non-violent action for civil rights in Birmingham, Alabama in 1963.

As the year 1963 drew near plans were being made to celebrate the one hundredth year since the Emancipation Proclamation as an anniversary of the liberation of blacks from bondage. However, there was great disillusionment on the part of the black population. Martin Luther King wrote that one hundred years after the Emancipation Proclamation blacks still lived, "on a lonely island of economic insecurity in the midst of a vast ocean of prosperity." Blacks were imprisoned both on the basis of colour and poverty. To King this kind of segregation was intolerable. Plans were laid for a massive non-violent direct-action campaign in Birmingham, Alabama, the most segregated city in the South. Local racists intimidated, mobbed, and even killed black people with impunity. The Commissioner of Public safety, "Bull Connor," defied the authority of the federal government and ruled with an iron hand.

Following detailed organization, protests took place; lunch-counter sit-ins, a march on City Hall, kneel-ins in churches, sit-ins in libraries and a massive boycott by blacks of the stores. Many people were arrested, but they went cheerfully and nonviolently. Finally, just before Easter, Martin Luther King and his co-leader, the Rev. Ralph Abernathy marched downtown into a "forbidden sector" and allowed themselves to be arrested. King was put in solitary confinement for twenty four hours and was not even allowed to see his wife until she called President Kennedy who intervened on his behalf.

In his famous "Letter from Birmingham Jail" in answer to some criticisms of his action on the part of eight clergymen from Birmingham, King responded with the rationale and faith basis for his action. In answer to the question as to why he came to Birmingham as an outsider to interfere in their affairs, he answers:

> I am in Birmingham because injustice is here. Just as the prophets of the eighth century B.C. left their villages and carried their, "thus saith the Lord" far beyond their home towns, so am I compelled to carry the gospel beyond my home town. . . Injustice anywhere is a threat to justice everywhere.

The white clergy had also asked, "Why sit-ins and direct action? Why not negotiation?" To this he replied that because calls for negotiation had failed, the goal of direct action was to bring about meaningful negotiations by causing such tension that the community is forced to face the issue.

King admits that it may seem paradoxical to urge people to obey the Supreme Court's decision outlawing segregation in the schools, but at the same time disobeying the laws of the city. The answer, he said, is that there are two types of laws: just and unjust laws. One has a moral responsibility to obey just laws, but also a moral responsibility to disobey unjust laws.

King was assassinated on April 4th, 1968 in Memphis, a martyr to the struggle for black liberation.

The life and words of Martin Luther King made a profound impression on me. Both his passion for the elimination of any form of oppression and his dedication to the use of active non-violence to bring about fundamental change have become guidelines for my own thinking and action. King's example made me eager to take part in public demonstrations for peace and against unjust situations both in Japan and in Canada.

GUSTAVO GUTIERREZ

An important encounter on my faith journey was when Fr. Tim Ryan introduced me to the writings of Gustavo Gutierrez in a guided reading course I took while on home assignment in 1975. In the introduction to his book, *A Theology of Liberation*, Gutierrez says:

> This book is an attempt at reflection, based on the Gospel and the experiences of men and women committed to the process of liberation in the oppressed and exploited land of Latin America. It is a theological reflection born of the experience of shared efforts to abolish the current unjust situation and build a different society, freer and more human.

Gutierrez makes a differentiation between the term "development" and "liberation." The thought among many western nations and church organizations has been, "If only the southern nations could be developed like the West their lives would be fine." However, "developmentalism," as he calls it, has become a pejorative term in Latin America, because, in spite of high hopes, it has failed to deliver. Poor countries have come to realize that their underdevelopment is only a by-product of the unequal relationship which exists between rich and poor countries. They came to realize that their own development will come about only through the struggle to break the domination of the rich countries and the elite within their own countries. This can only be accomplished with a profound transformation of the property system, access to power of the exploited class, and a social revolution that would allow for the change to a new society. For this reason "liberation" is seen to be a more appropriate term than development.

Gutierrez proposes that liberation is the more appropriate term not only in a sociological sense but also in a Biblical sense. The Bible does not speak of the need for kinder task-masters in Egypt for the Israelite slaves but of their liberation. The prophets thunder about the exploitation of the poor and disadvantaged and call for a transformation, a new economic and social order.

So fundamental did Gutierrez and other Latin American liberation theologians consider the need for concrete action on behalf of the poor that they coined the term, "God's preferential option for the poor." To them the God of the Old and New Testaments was a God who is revealed as standing on the side of all who are poor and exploited, and we are called upon to do the same.

There were those within the Latin American church who criticized liberation theologians for being too political. However, Gutierrez points out that supporting the status quo is also being very much political. Is the church going to use its influence to support the established order, as it has done in the past, or give its support to the revolutionary process which brings liberation to the vast majority of the population?

In many Latin American countries, priests who took up the cause of the liberation of the poor, were eliminated by murder or "disappearances" by ruthless dictators. Archbishop Romero of El Salvador, who was murdered March 24th, 1980 while conducting a mass in the Cathedral, was only the most prominent.

In spite of persecution, liberation theology became very popular throughout Latin America, especially among priests and church workers who were working with the poor. Almost spontaneously thousands of Bible study groups called "base communities" sprang up throughout the region. Base communities were groups that used Bible study to relate the Bible to social conditions and encouraged the participants to free themselves from the oppression in which they found themselves. Despite the obvious response throughout most of Latin America to the message of the liberation theologians, most of the hierarchy of the Roman Catholic church has repudiated the work of the liberation theologians. Even in Protestant theological seminaries, liberation theology did not become mainstream. At best, courses in liberation theology were offered as options. I look upon the ignoring of the central thrust of liberation theology by the churches a betrayal of a fundamental message of the Bible itself.

I believe liberation theology has a relevance for our own society here in Canada where the gap between the rich and the poor continues to increase and rich corporations dictate more and more of our governments' policies. The churches here should also be in the forefront in the struggle for liberation.

KOREAN MINJUN THEOLOGY
One of the liberation theologies that developed in Asia was the Minjun Theology of Korea. The Korean word "Minjun" is a term referring especially to the oppressed and suffering people of Korea. Minjun Theology is the theological reflection on the experiences of Christian students, labourers, the press, farmers, writers and others who had experienced persecutions and court trials for the sake of conscience in Korea in the 1970s.

I have a particular interest in the birth of this theology of liberation because Japan is in close proximity to Korea. In 1965 our family made a short trip to attend a mission conference of Canadian missionaries working in Korea. We were distressed by the contrast in living standards between Japan and Korea. This period was at the height of the mass student demonstrations against the signing of the Japan-Korea Treaty that they feared would again bring Korea under more Japanese control. We saw lying in the streets the stones that had been thrown by the students against the military. I kept in touch with Canadian missionaries working in Korea and tried to keep abreast of the struggles against the repressive regimes which followed.

My concern for Korea was heightened by the fact that I have a daughter-in-law, Suzuko, who, although born and raised in Japan, is of Korean nationality. Through her and her family I was made aware, not only of the discrimination that Korean people faced in Japan, but of the sorry tale of the Japanese occupation years and of persecution of the South Korean people by the corrupt Korean government in the post-war period.

I found that the Korean people's struggle for liberation, personally and nationally, can best be interpreted through the eyes of those associated with Minjun Theology. David Kwang-sun Suh describes the origin of Minjun Theology in this way:

> Minjun Theology has developed out of the Korean Christian's intuitive and acute awareness of the essence of the Christian message as both political and religious - as the good news and hope for liberation of the oppressed people.

The Korean people have a long history of oppression. In 1905 Korea was taken over by Japan as a "protectorate," and in 1910, Japan formally annexed Korea. The people of Korea lost their country and became enslaved subjects to Japanese rule. All Korean social and political organizations were closed down. The Koreans were unable to publish newspapers in their own language, or teach Korean history or culture. They were coerced into worshipping the Japanese Emperor and were given Japanese names instead of Korean. They were also prohibited from speaking Korean in schools or public places. The military seized lands and took over fishery rights, and timber and mining rights. In spite of oppression Koreans continued to struggle for their freedom and independence.

In 1945, Korea was liberated from the Japanese colonial rule, but this liberation was not by their own efforts. Korea became a victim of the cold war and Korea was divided into two parts.

I do not have the knowledge as to what happened to the Christian church in the north, so I must confine my remarks to the Republic of Korea. The United States assumed Japan's imperial role in the south and brought in Syngman Rhee from exile in the States as the U.S. approved leader. Rhee's regime, marked by anti-communist frenzy, police brutality, electoral fraud and bribery led to unrest and mass student demonstrations. When Rhee became an embarrassment the U.S. decided to depose him. With U.S. backing, General Park Chung Hee initiated a military coup and arrested student leaders who were demonstrating in support of Korean re-unification. Park became even more repressive than Rhee. He created anti-communist laws under which he arrested and eliminated all opposition.

Under his tight control, foreign companies took advantage of Korea's anti-union and anti-strike laws to set up factory assembly lines paying starvation wages.

It was under these forms of oppression that Minjun Theology was born to fight for liberation and a free and democratic society. There were many Korean Christian leaders who had a part in promoting Minjun Theology. I would like to hold up the life and writings of Kim Chi Ha, a poet who endured imprisonment and suffering because of his poetry and writings, as one who most clearly exemplified the spirit of Minjun Theology.

Kim Chi Ha was born in 1941 in South Korea. He entered Seoul National University in 1959 and in 1964 took part in student movement activities opposing government policies. He was imprisoned and tortured. In 1970 he published his parable-poem "Five Bandits," about the injustice and corruption of the privileged classes in South Korea. Park arrested him again on the grounds that he had violated the Anti-Communist Law. He was bailed out of prison, having contracted tuberculosis. In 1971, he organized a demonstration by six hundred Catholics in his native province of Cholla. He was arrested again in 1974 after having published a poem "Cry of the People" which spread throughout Korea in pamphlet form. This time he was subjected to military court martial and accused of violating the National Security Law and was sentenced to death, but his sentence was later commuted to life imprisonment. An international committee to "Save Kim Chi Ha" was formed which included Jean Paul Sartre and Noam Chomsky and resulted in his unexpected release from prison for a time, only to be re-arrested in 1975 when he was tortured into admitting he was a Communist, a statement he later retracted. A later trial added seven years to his life sentence.

Kim Chi Ha had an indomitable spirit that imprisonment and cruel torture could not overcome. In a letter to the "National Priests Association for the Realization of Justice" written in prison and smuggled out of his cell, he shares something of the ordeal he was enduring:

> I am in solitary confinement in a dark cell and forbidden to write or read, even Scripture. I spend the day in meditation, surrounded by these gloomy walls. Nonetheless my spirits are closer to the Lord than ever before... Buoyed by your call for freedom, my soul has repeatedly burst out of my cell and over the high prison walls to be with you in the desperate struggle. As long as the Lord is at my side and you continue your dauntless movement out there, I have no misgivings about this tribulation the Lord has presented me as a sign of his divine will.

The essence of his minjun spirit is revealed in his "declaration of conscience" that he also had smuggled out of his cell:

> I cannot describe this Promised Land in detail. My task is to fight on until the people hold in their own hands the power to shape their destiny. I want a victory for real democracy, complete freedom of speech. In this sense, I am a radical democrat and libertarian. I am also a Catholic, one of the oppressed citizens of the Republic of Korea, and a young man who loathes privilege, corruption and dictatorial power.

Kim Chi Ha claims that the greatest influence on his thinking has been his participation since 1971 in the Korean Christian movement for human rights (the Minjun Theology movement). This experience convinced him that the Korean tradition of resistance and revolution with its unique vitality under incredibly negative circumstances are precious materials for a new form of human liberation.

Some of Kim's strongest statements are made in his poems and plays that brought down the wrath of the government. I find in these poetic words of Kim Chi Ha the message of a modern Scripture, speaking the words and spirit of Jesus for our own time. Kim expresses the truth and spirit of liberation theology to Korea and the Third World, but his message also speaks to the corruption and insensitivity of people in our own nation as well.

The struggle of the Korean people, inspired partly by Minjun Theology and the dedication of people like Kim Chi Ha was not without its reward. In 1973 the dictator President Park Chung Chi was shot by his chief bodyguard. After his death there were several short term Presidents who continued persecution until there was a mass uprising in the city of Kwang Ju in which many protestors were massacred. The protests finally led to the emergence of a democratic government. In 1980 Kim Chi Ha's sentence was commuted and he was released from prison.

Several years earlier, in 1973, a Korean political dissident, Kim Dae Jung, was kidnapped in Japan by Korean government secret service agents for campaigning against the Park government. He was taken by ship to Korea and put under house arrest in Seoul. After his release in 1980 he became active in politics and was eventually elected President. Kim Dae Jung introduced many progressive policies. He also has initiated peace talks with North Korea and arranged for family visits between people of the North and South.

Kim Chi Ha, now feeling vindicated for his efforts for the liberation of the people of South Korea, lives quietly in the country town of Ilsan, not far from Seoul. He still publishes an occasional poem.

Korea and the whole world owes Kim Chi Ha a great deal of gratitude for his dedication and the suffering he was prepared to endure for the liberation of his people. In his life he expressed the true spirit of Minjun Theology.

JAMES CONE AND THE BLACK THEOLOGY OF LIBERATION

My first encounter with James H. Cone was through reading his book, *Liberation, A Black Theology of Liberation*, during my home assignment year of 1975-76. I found his book stimulating and thought-provoking. He gave me social and theological insights into, not only the oppression of blacks in the United States, but also the oppression of all marginalized people of the world. Many years later, when I was on the staff of the Prairie Christian Training Centre in Fort Qu'Appelle, Saskatchewan, I arranged for him to lead a weekend seminar on liberation theology. What made this event even more meaningful was the fact that many of the participants were Canadian First Nations students studying for the Christian ministry at the Dr. Jesse Saulteaux Training Centre. They were able to draw the parallels between the discrimination against blacks in the United States and the history of oppression of native peoples in Canada.

I remember distinctively a workshop in which groups were asked to put on short skits depicting some aspect of oppression with which they were acquainted. The native group put on a hilarious but also very hard-hitting skit on residential schools. In their skit they reversed the roles. The natives were running a residential school for whites. Among the things that were required of them was that they must all wear their hair in braids, they were to speak Cree only, and would be punished if caught speaking English. They were isolated in the school and were only allowed to return home once a year. It was a vivid learning experience for the rest of us.

We found James Cone to be a knowledgeable and personable leader. His grasp of both the condition of oppressed people, and the Biblical and theological basis for concrete action were impressive. He was a Professor of Systematic Theology at Union Theological Seminary in New York and by this time had written five books on black liberation theology.

James Cone grew up in Bearden, Arkansas, during the 1940s and 1950s. In Bearden, a much segregated community, he encountered the harsh realities of white injustice that was inflicted daily upon the black community. At the same time his faith was nourished in the Macedonia American Methodist Episcopal Church which, he says, sustained his personhood and dignity, in spite of white people's brutality.

It was out of this background and tension that his black theology of liberation grew. In church, home and school he was taught to resist oppression and injustice. He was strongly influenced by his father who defended his rights and spoke the truth, regardless of the risks. His mother was one of the pillars of the Macedonia church and a firm believer in God's justice. He was nourished by his family and the church to think that God was on their side against the satanic force of white supremacy.

When he went to Garrett Biblical Institute in Evanston, Illinois in 1958, he first believed that in the northern U.S. race relations would be much different. His naivete was rudely shattered when he went into a white barbershop and sat down in a chair only to be told by a barber, "We don't cut niggers' hair in this place." He said later, "I have never really quite gotten over that experience."

In his first book, *Black Theology and Black Power*, Cone declares:

> White racism is a disease. No excuse can be made for it; we blacks can only oppose it with every ounce of our humanity. When black children die of rat bites, and black men suffer because meaning has been sapped from their existence, and black women weep because family stability is gone, how can anyone appeal to "reason." Black power then is an expression of hope, not hope that whites will change the structure of oppression, but hope in the humanity of black people.

Cone says that "Freedom Now" has been and is still the slogan of all civil rights groups.

Black power is a part of this ongoing movement for liberation. Cone insists that since black Christians have grown up with the image of Jesus and God as white, the only real way for them to know that God is with them is to see Jesus and God as black. In *Black Theology and Black Power*, he asks:

> Where does Christ lead his people? Where indeed if not in the ghetto. He meets the blacks where they are and becomes one of them. We see him with his black face and big black hands lounging on a street corner.

Blackness in the racial situation in the United States becomes a symbol for all kinds of oppression. Christ himself was oppressed and because he is oppressed he is also black. The way for the church is to follow Christ, going where suffering is and becoming black also. What does this mean in practical terms for white churches? It means a radical reorientation of their style in the world towards blacks. It means that white churches must change sides, giving up their neutrality and identifying with the oppressed blacks, even tasting the sting of oppression themselves.

LIBERATION AND THE KINGDOM OF GOD

I have earlier spoken of what the Kingdom of God meant to Edis Fairbairn and Toyohiko Kagawa. They spoke of the kingdom as a new social order based on justice and peace. Kagawa in particular sought to establish that kingdom through labour unions, farmers' cooperatives and through working with the poor in the slums. Cone would recognize these actions as a part of the kingdom but he is more specific as to what was required in a society marked by massive discrimination against black people. He says that the kingdom is not the attainment of material security, nor is it mystical communion with the divine. It has to do with the quality of one's existence in which the individual realizes that persons are more important than property. It means black people shaking off the chains of white oppression.

Although Cone talks mainly about the oppression of black people, he does also include other oppressed people of the world. He says that the oppressed are people in the black ghettos, the Indian reservations, the Spanish barrios and other places where whiteness has created misery. Cone makes it perfectly clear that because white people as a class have been so closely bound with black enslavement, and that enslavement still continues in so many ways, the hope of true reconciliation is very bleak. He declares that there can be no forgiveness without repentance, and no repentance without the gift of faith, to struggle with and for the freedom of the oppressed.

The road ahead for anyone of a dominant race in any society where oppression is rampant is not easy, but it is worth the sacrifice. James Cone raises for me many of the theological issues with which I am still struggling. How do we take a stand against injustice that is endemic in a society or even within the church? Which side is God on and how do I align myself with God's purposes? How can we as individuals or as a church repent of past and present injustices, for instance against First Nations people in Canada?

FEMINIST LIBERATION THEOLOGY
Until I began reading some of the works of feminist liberation theologians during my 1975-6 home assignment, I was not fully aware of discrimination against women in Canada and around the world. I deplored the fact that in Canada women's salaries were only about 70% of that of men in the same categories, but didn't know what we could do about it. The United Church had opened ordination for women in the thirties and Doreen had a very fruitful ministry on the Orville pastoral charge. I was not really aware of the magnitude of the issue of women in poverty or of violence against women.

On moving to Japan, I found patriarchy and the position of women in society so much worse than in Canada that I tended to look on Canada as a role model. One incident which happened shortly after we moved to Nayoro illustrates the lack of recognition that women had in Japanese society.

Mr. Tamura, minister of the Nayoro church, told me that I was invited to a dinner at a restaurant owned by one of the church members. I took it for granted that since both Doreen and myself had been appointed as cooperating missionaries to the Nayoro church, Doreen was also invited. Doreen was delighted, and looked forward to getting out for a dinner in town. However, as she was busily getting herself and one-year-old baby Dennis ready to go to the supper we received a phone call from Mrs. Tamura. She had heard that Doreen was also preparing to go, so she informed us that, no, the invitation had been only for myself. Doreen was dejected and I was angry, but what could we do about it without creating a scene at the beginning of our ministry? From then on we did work at trying to break down prejudice against women in Japan, and tried to set a role model in the home. Some of the husbands joked that we were making it hard for them since their wives complained that they weren't helping around the home as much as I did.

In the Three Love Schools for farm young people, we called our two day summer events "homemaking parties" where we dealt with partnership in homes and the role of women and men in their homes. As I read books by Rosemary Ruether and Letty Russell I discovered whole new dimensions of the various forms of oppression experienced by women not only overseas but also in Canada and the United States.

ROSEMARY RUETHER
I had the privilege of meeting Rosemary Ruether when the Prairie Christian Training Centre invited her to be a workshop leader on Feminist Liberation Theology for a weekend study conference. She was very articulate and her lectures were based on competent scholarship.

In Rosemary Ruether's book, *Liberation Theology*, I discovered, first of all, the ways in which the oppression of women had been reinforced by narrow and literalist Biblical interpretations. In a chapter entitled, "Is Christianity Misogynist? The Failure of Women's Liberation in the Church" she delineates the ways in which women and women's bodies have been denigrated during the years of the Christian era. Whereas, in the Bible, many women were numbered among Jesus' followers, and some of the leaders in the early New Testament church were women, that changed as the church became more established. For instance, Tertullian, a second century theologian, speaks of woman's role as "the Devil's gateway" and sees her nature permanently marked by her special guilt in causing the fall of man, leading up to the necessity for the death of Christ.

St. Augustine, also a second century theologian, sees the cause of the fall to lie more on the natural inferiority of women. To women he attributed the "carnal" traits, pettiness, sensuality, materialism and maliciousness, while to men are attributed the virtues of chastity, patience, wisdom, temperance, fortitude and justice. To all the church fathers sex is a dirty word. Woman is the temptress and as such the sexual act can never be thought of as a vehicle of love, but only to be used for the purpose of procreation. The highest form of salvation for a woman under this order of things was to choose the life of virginity.

It seems preposterous that such a doctrine of man and woman should hold sway for so many centuries within the Roman Catholic Church. It has been one of the ways in which women have been subjugated by men. Its effects are still to be seen not only in the Catholic Church but also in Protestant churches. For instance, I heard of a Methodist missionary who insisted that his wife get changed for bed in the closet and that sex should only take place at night, in the dark and under the covers.

Because of the patriarchy evident in the Bible and narrow literalist interpretations of Biblical texts many feminists have rejected the Bible altogether as a basis for liberation. Rosemary Ruether does not repudiate the Bible but calls for a re-assessment of the Jesus' story as a way of discovering a theological basis for Christian feminism. She explains:

> Modern Jesus scholarship has radically stripped the Jesus story of its dogmatic accretions, revealing a Jesus whose life continues to strike a responsive chord for feminist liberation theology - namely, a man, (not lord, but brother) who dissented from the religious and social systems of domination that marginalized the poor and the despised, most notably women. He incurred the wrath of the religious and political authorities for these subversive teachings and practices, and they sought to silence him by publicly torturing him to death.

When I came back to Canada after a six-year absence in 1975 I was still referring to God using the male pronoun. I was impressed by Rosemary Ruether's exposition of the Bible's use of images for God other than the male, patriarchal ones. For instance, when the Hebrew Scriptures want to portray the unconditional love and immense compassion of Yahweh, they turn to maternal imagery. Isaiah pictures the Lord crying out like a woman in labour. Female imagery is used in describing Wisdom as an offspring of Yahweh, cooperating in the work of creation and serving as the representative of the divine presence in the world. Throughout her writings Ruether employs this Hebrew imagery, describing God as the liberator who fights for the injustices borne by women, and as the Mother who nurtures them to full personhood, and the Holy Wisdom who guides them to truth and meaning.

In the Gospels, she points to stories that use both genders to describe God's activity in the world. For instance, in Luke's Gospel, God's work in establishing the Kingdom is referred to both as a farmer sowing seed and a woman leavening bread. Jesus broke social taboos by speaking to women in public and by engaging in religious dialogue with Mary and Martha. God, Ruether insists, is beyond gender. I fully embraced her arguments and now I do not use gender related vocabulary when referring to the Divine.

Although Ruether is highly critical of the institutional church she does not repudiate it altogether but calls for a creative dialectic between feminist based communities and the institutional church. This enables them to use the institution creatively, while gradually transforming it into a genuine sign of liberated humanity and a useful instrument in the battle against all patriarchal institutions.

The philosophy of working through basic communities in order to transform the church has been a part of my own approach. Wherever I have gone, I have tried to connect with or reproduce what I called the small group "cell" models seeking to transform the church This approach has had some positive results that have kept me within the church, in spite of often becoming disillusioned and frustrated by many of its antiquated doctrines and practices.

LETTY M. RUSSELL

Letty Russell was also one of the Feminist Liberation theologians that I read during my first exposure to feminist liberation. Whereas Rosemary Ruether might be described as a theologian's theologian, Letty Russell, out of her own wide experience of working with liberation issues, develops some of the more practical aspects. She wrote out of her involvement with the YWCA in both the United States and India, and her pastoral experience of ministry among the poor, the blacks and the

Puerto Ricans in the East Harlem Protestant Parish. At the time of writing her book, *Human Liberation in a Feminist Perspective - a Theology*, she was Professor of the Practice of Theology at Yale Divinity School. Russell describes Feminist Liberation Theology in this way:

> Like Third World liberation theology, feminist theology is written out of an experience of oppression in society. It interprets the search for salvation as a journey toward freedom, as a process of self-liberation in community with others in the light of hope in God's promise. Together with other people searching for freedom, women wish to speak of the hope that is in them. They want to tell the world that they are a part of God's plan of human liberation.

Telling the world that they are part of God's plan of human liberation, involves an education/action process. Taking her cue from Paulo Friere she calls for a "conscientization" process both for women themselves to be awakened to a recognition of the nature of their oppression, and for men to have their eyes opened to ways in which they are consciously or unconsciously oppressing women.

For women there is always a danger of buying into the patriarchal system. This can be done in two ways. First, she may accept the traditional role of her culture which can be characterized as "the happy slave." She sees herself being fulfilled in the accepted role of mother, secretary, servant or sex symbol. She may even become defensive seeing "women's lib" as a threat.

Another way in which women may become blind to their own oppression in society is to emulate the oppressor. They devote all energy and attention into getting ahead within the highly competitive society in what is often considered "men's" world.

Russell warns that the manner in which education or conscientization takes place is very important. Recruitment of new members to the liberation cause can take the form of feminist propaganda designed to create women in the one-size-fits-all feminist image, instead of letting the love of God become incarnated in each individual woman's life.

When it comes to raising the consciousness of men to the discrimination and oppression of women in our society, the task becomes even more difficult. The recommended approach is through dialogue, but dialogue with oppressor groups can only happen when there is a situation of equality and trust. "If you want to talk to me, take your foot off my neck." Russell recommends that the oppressed develop their own power base of mutual support, new identity, and new possibility for collective action.

As men become aware of the fact that they do belong to an oppressor class they too can strive to free themselves, and to join forces with women to bring about liberation for both women and men. Once I awakened to the nature of the oppression of women, I have called myself a "male feminist" and have sought to be an advocate on their behalf.

Russell also deals with the task of opening up the church for significant leadership roles. She points out that pressure for the liberation of women in societies around the world is exposing the sexist practices in the church. A persistent chorus of voices, both male and female, is calling for a new look at the meaning of ministry and mission in a world calling for justice and liberation of all people. Many churches still exclude women from ordination, but even in those churches that have opened up to the ordination of women there are still significant barriers to the full recognition of their talents and abilities. I heard the wives of two ministers of the United Church remark that they preferred male ministers because they had better voices for the pulpit. We still have a long way to go in most churches toward full equality among the leadership.

New models of ministry which Russell proposes resonate with my conception of a ministry belonging to the whole people of God, with a wide variety of roles based on God's mission of liberation in the world. She calls for a continual process of action and reflection which she refers to as "doing theology." She envisages new models of servanthood that would begin with the assumption that all the people of God are ministers, and each one needs help in finding ways to develop his or her gifts for service.

Letty Russell challenges us to work for a world where men and women are equal and where each could express his or her lifestyle in a variety of ways. She envisions a world in which the oppressed peoples of the world could move together to eliminate barriers of sex, race, and class that deprive people of their opportunity to live out the life of freedom. A deeper understanding of Feminist Liberation Theology has helped me to make one of my goals the elimination of barriers in all sectors of society.

THE ROLE OF LIBERATION THEOLOGIES

Liberation theologies have played an important role in giving a new breath of life to traditional theological interpretations and a new perspective on the relationship of God and of spirituality in the world. When I studied theology in college, much of it was very academic and had little relation to world issues. We were told that we must be non-partisan and always examine both sides. When examining theories and doctrines it is necessary to have an open mind to allow for change and growth. But on issues of life and death, discrimination, oppression and the dignity of the human person, it is always necessary to take sides.

The liberation theologies I have examined here, and the ones which had the greatest influence on my thinking and actions have many common bases, each offering different emphases. The Latin American liberation theologies speak to issues of political and social oppression. They make much of social analysis based not on Marxism, but on central Biblical positions of justice and liberation that have been too often ignored among theologians because they challenge the status quo.

Black Liberation theologians deal with the specific scandal of racism, a blight on the body politic, not only in the United States but also in many other societies. The Biblical message is clear - discrimination and oppression on the basis of race or colour is intolerable and must be eradicated.

The Minjun Theology of Korea, as represented by Kim Chi Ha, shows the way in which a people's spirit can resist foreign occupation and political corruption in dictatorial societies. Kim Chi Ha's courage and indomitable spirit in the face of torture and the threat of death shows the depths of dedication sometimes required.

Feminist Liberation Theologies opened up an area of oppression that had become systemic in almost all societies and yet which had been largely ignored by male-dominated societies and churches. They lift up a basic principle that the initiative for liberation must come first from the oppressed communities themselves. However, a corollary is that at the same time oppressed communities also need advocates from the oppressor groups to give support and help. The leaders of liberation movements have been pioneers in developing principles and actions for human liberation which can be applied, not only to these particular examples of oppression, but to many other societies and groups crying out for freedom throughout the world.

GAY/LESBIAN LIBERATION: MY OWN AWAKENING

One of the sectors of our society in need of liberation of which I was unaware for many years was that of the suffering and oppression of our gay and lesbian brothers and sisters. Much of their suffering has been caused by the condemnatory attitude of the churches and those who called themselves Christian. The issue of sexual orientations was scarcely talked about while I was growing up except in jokes. My first real recognition of the immensity of the injustice that had been perpetuated through the years came from personal experience. In Japan we recruited young people to come for periods of two to three years to teach English Conversation in the Dohoku Centre English School. Some of these lived with us during their stay in Japan. One of these, Alan McLean, a graduate of Trent University, became like one of the family over his three year stay in the early seventies, in Nayoro.

After returning to Canada for theological studies, he wrote telling us that, after much struggle, he had come to realize that he was gay and that he hoped that wouldn't change our relationship. We wrote that our love would always be with him, that he had been like a son to us and we would fully support him. We also said we would like to learn more.

Alan sent us some books. As we read we became more and more horrified by the injustice that is heaped upon people of differing sexual orientations. We also read about the narrow interpretations of a few isolated passages in the Bible that have condemned generations of gay and lesbian people to discrimination, persecution and even death. The much more prominent passages in the Bible calling for love and acceptance of all people had been completely overlooked.

The opportunity to try to do something about this injustice came when we returned to Canada and I accepted a staff position at the Prairie Christian Training Centre (P.C.T.C.) in Fort Qu'Appelle, Saskatchewan in 1982. I found that the Centre had already done considerable work in preparing a study guide for churches on sexual orientation. They were now wanting to expand their involvement by holding a special week-end conference at the Centre for gay and lesbian Christians. Before we could do this, however, we felt that, because there might be considerable fall-out from this action among some church members, we would have to consult the Board of the Centre. At a Board meeting, we conducted a workshop dealing with the issue of sexual orientation and the possible negative and positive responses that might be engendered by holding such a conference. After considerable discussion the members of the Board said, "We know there may be criticism, but because we think it is the right thing to do, go ahead and carry out the programme."

The event was advertised throughout the United Churches of Saskatchewan and Manitoba, along with other programs of P.C.T.C. for the spring of 1983. Gordon Jardine, the Staff member with the most skills in facilitation, was the only heterosexual to be included. About fifteen gay and lesbian participants registered. Most of them were not even "out" to their own families, let alone to their churches. They came with considerable trepidation. Some even felt uncomfortable having

Gordon there. However, by the time the weekend was over, they were thrilled with the experience of sharing with gay and lesbian friends and appreciated tremendously Gordon's facilitation. They said, "We want to do this again next year, but this time we would also like to invite supportive heterosexual friends." We called these annual events "Finding Ways to Care." After Gordon had left the Centre staff, I also assisted in the leadership and found these events to be among the highlights of my experiences at P.C.T.C.

After the first event my task was to answer critical letters. There were about fifteen letters, some very critical of our action and some threatening to withdraw support from P.C.T.C. I tried to answer these with as much sympathy and understanding as I could. I pointed out what we saw as the Biblical basis for our action and the need for love and acceptance. Wilma Wessel, the third member of our program staff, took up organizing support groups for gays and lesbians in Saskatchewan and Manitoba. Within a few years the gay and lesbian Christians had organized a group which they called "Affirm," affirming the rights of gay and lesbian Christians in the United Church. Wilma helped to organize groups of supporters called "Friends of Affirm." At the same time similar groups were being organized in other parts of Canada. These two groups eventually amalgamated to become "Affirm United."

The United Church central offices sent out study kits to the churches dealing with issues of sexuality, including homosexuality. Resolutions were sent to the General Council of the United Church from some of the United Church Presbyteries and Conferences calling for recognition of full rights for gay and lesbian Christians. In the face of considerable opposition a resolution was passed by the 1988 General Council which stated in part:

> all persons, regardless of their sexual orientation, are welcome to be or become members of the United Church and all members are eligible to be considered for ministry positions.

When this resolution was taken back to local churches there was considerable furore in some congregations. Some members withdrew their memberships and a few local churches left the United Church over this issue. However, the United Church felt that this was the right thing to do in spite of the pain it caused within some congregations. It was found that this action was not all negative. Some people who had given up on the church were attracted back into the church by what they felt to be a courageous stand, and some members of other denominations joined the United Church because of its inclusiveness.

There is still a long way to go toward full liberation for our homosexual brothers and sisters, both in church and society, but some progress is being made. I am glad for the opportunity to have been in the front line of this struggle for this aspect of human liberation. But this is also an ongoing process. After coming to the Peterborough area Doreen and I helped to form a local Affirm group which met monthly in our Lakefield home. After Doreen's death in 1992, this group continued for a time in my new wife Sheila's and my home in Peterborough until the group grew too large and decided to have monthly worship services in St. Andrew's United Church. These meetings for worship and fellowship for gays and lesbians, their families and friends have been a real source of inspiration for all who have participated. Leadership is shared, so there is a wide variety of informal worship and a mutual sharing and support for all who attend. This is one place in which Sheila and I, and all who participate, find real spiritual nourishment and close friendships in a new style of church.

I find it a challenge to be involved in the struggle for the liberation of many people in the community and the world - the struggle for the poor and disadvantaged; the emancipation of people of colour in our midst; the fight for the rights of Canada's First Nations and for aboriginal groups in many countries; the struggle for equal rights for women; the full acceptance of gay and lesbian people and their same-sex partnerships. Working for the liberation of these and other groups are all part of my faith odyssey that always changes but never ends.

11

DIALOGUE WITH PEOPLE OF OTHER FAITHS

Living in Japan, where less than one percent of the people are Christian, I found it necessary to explore the origins and nature of other faiths. I did this in two ways, by getting to know personally people of other faiths and doing a rather extensive study of Japanese religions. I subscribed to a quarterly magazine which engaged in inter-faith dialogue and contained articles written by members of the various religions and sects. I found these articles greatly helped my attempts to understand both the religions and the psyche of Japanese people.

Japan's two traditional religions are Shinto and Buddhism. Most Japanese families identify themselves with Shinto shrines, Buddhist temples or one of the many "new religions" of which I will speak later. This does not mean that all of them know a great deal about their religions or engage regularly in their practices. Often when we asked young people what religion they belonged to they would answer, "My family religion is Buddhist, or Shinto, but personally I don't have any religion." Especially in the immediate post-war period this was the attitude of many of the youth who had been disillusioned by the propaganda of the war period when state Shinto had been enforced on everyone. This was one reason why many of the Japanese turned to the new religions and also why some young people came to the churches looking for some new direction in life.

THE SHINTO RELIGION

When we moved to Nayoro in 1953 our house was built on the northern edge of town. Our closest neighbours, the Kurisu family, had a dairy farm and were members of the Nayoro Shinto shrine. They never talked much about their faith. They paid their shrine dues and observed some of the festival days.

The fact that we were Christian never made any difference to them. They welcomed us with open arms, bringing us gifts of corn and other farm produce. Dennis loved to walk down to the farm to see the cows and to ride on the two wheeled, horse-drawn wagon when they took their milk to the local milk plant. Mrs. Kurisu urged Doreen to start a cooking class where neighbours and friends could learn western cooking. Since, for a time, we had the only telephone in the neighbourhood, they would frequently come to the house to use the telephone. We enjoyed many friendly conversations with the whole family.

Some months after we arrived, they asked if I could take them to the local cemetery in our Jeep to hold a memorial service for a son who had died in the war. He had been serving in the Japanese army in Manchuria and at the end of the war he had been taken prisoner and had died in a Russian prison camp. His ashes had been brought back and interred in the Nayoro cemetery. A Japanese custom is to hold a memorial ceremony on the anniversary of a person's death as the spirit of the deceased is thought to be especially present on this date. I was glad to help them with the transportation. They had a simple ceremony, lighting a candle, placing a dish with some of their son's favourite foods beside the gravestone, clapping their hands and saying a prayer.

Several years later their daughter, Sumako, became interested in the Christian faith and attended the Nayoro church for a time. The family did not object to her going to the church where they thought she would get good teaching. However, when she spoke of the possibility of joining the church they discouraged her and she decided not to be baptized. After we had returned to Canada, Mr. Kurisu Senior, the patriarch of the family, died. When I went back to Japan in 1988, we called on Sumako and she asked if we would go to her parental home and say a Christian prayer in memory of her father in front of the Shinto "godshelf" where her father was memorialized. I thought that this request was significant, since it indicated her continuing interest in Christianity and her sense that God is present in all religions. In my prayer I gave thanks for Mr. Kurisu's life and friendship and prayed for the comfort of the whole family. I was happy to have the opportunity to participate in this little prayer service with Sumako. We were exceedingly grateful for the friendship and support the Kurisu family had given us all the time we were living in Nayoro.

"Shinto" means "the way of the gods." It is the most ancient of the Japanese religions and is based on a mythology with many animistic elements. It recognizes spirits in the trees, the grass, the rivers and the sky, and honours the beauty of nature. This tradition is one of the reasons many Japanese people have such a love for nature and appreciation for beauty in simple things. Shinto shrines are almost always set in a beautiful grove of trees.

The Emperor of Japan was, according to ancient tradition, descended from the "sun god" and was in the past revered as a sort of divine figure. During the 1930s the military government made use of Shinto by declaring it a national religion and demanding that all Japanese citizens, even the citizens of the conquered nations of Korea and Taiwan, worship the Emperor as a divine figure. School children were daily forced to pledge their allegiance to the photo of the Emperor and to sing the national anthem. Soldiers were urged to offer their lives in dedication to the Emperor and to their country. In these ways the military was able to pervert Shinto for its own nationalistic purposes. At the end of the war, with the establishment of a new constitution that guaranteed freedom of religion and separation of church and state, Shinto lost its privileged position and had to maintain itself as an independent religion. Several attempts have been made to get state financial support for the Yasukuni Shrine in Tokyo where the war dead are memorialized, but this has always been strongly opposed by both Buddhist and Christian groups. However, most towns and villages still observe Shinto Festival days in the summer with colourful parades in which portable shrines are carried through the town to the beating of drums and dancing.

THE BUDDHIST RELIGION

My closest personal association with the Buddhist tradition was with the Sasakis, a father and son who were Buddhist priests in the Tokoji Temple in Nayoro. What impressed me most, when I got to know them, was their great love of nature. All around the temple grounds they had planted a wide variety of native wild flowers. The senior priest, Ryushu Sasaki, had a hobby of painting wild flowers. Once when we visited him he was busy painting wild flowers on post cards. He gave us one and then explained that he was painting these cards to have them ready to be sent out as an announcement of his funeral. However, he joked, "I keep giving them away so that I don't have time to die." I recently heard that in March of 2002 Ryushu Sasaki had died at over 90 years of age. I give thanks for his life and for an opportunity to know such a dedicated and spiritual person.

In conversations with both the older and younger priest I discovered that they knew a great deal about the Bible and respected its teachings. The attitude of most of the Buddhist people whom I have met is that they are ready to accept truth wherever it is to be found. In 1988 I took a tour group to Japan and when in Nayoro took them to visit the temple. There I asked Ryuji Sasaki to give a talk about their temple and some of the basic teachings of their branch of the Buddhist faith. Rob Witmer, my successor in the mission work in Nayoro, did the interpretation. Although the concepts may have been a bit difficult for the group they enjoyed the visit to the temple and found the introduction to the Buddhist faith fascinating.

Besides his regular work at the temple, Ryuji, the younger priest, is very active in community affairs. The first time I met him was at the Nayoro/Lindsay twinning committee, of which he has been an active member. Over the years we have become close friends. When Ryuji and his father heard we were returning to Canada in 1981, Ryuji brought to our house a beautiful framed water colour of a dog-toothed violet and a colourful marsh plant painted by his father. On the back the father had written, vertically in the Japanese style, the English word "PRESENT." I treasure this painting and have it hanging on the wall in front of my desk as I write.

There are many traditional Buddhist sects in Japan, having their origins in China. The earliest came in the 6th century

A.D. and adapted to Japanese cultural patterns. The Tendai and Shingon sects were established in the 9th century. Buddhism became a popular religion in the 12th and 13th centuries with the establishment of the Jodo (Pure land) sects, Zen Buddhism, and Nichiren Buddhism. The Pure Land Sects emphasize salvation by faith in the Amida Buddha and the repetition of the phrase "Namu Amida Butsu" (Honour to the Buddha of Boundless Light). Zen Buddhism emphasizes mystic, intuitive insight gained through a discipline of meditation. Out of Zen has grown the art of flower arranging (ikebana), tea ceremony and archery, which have had a big influence on the cultural life of Japan. Nichiren Buddhism, based on devotion to the Lotus Sutra, is more exclusive and more active in winning "converts" to its cause. Out of Nichiren Buddhism has grown two of the most widespread of the "new religions," Soka Gakkai and Rissho Koseikai, of which I will say more later.

JAPANESE NEW RELIGIONS

Japanese "new religions" are ones that for the most part have grown up within the last one hundred years, many of them in post-war Japan. They are usually centred around a charismatic leader, who has made a break from the traditional religions. They often try to combine elements of Shinto, Buddhist and also sometimes Christianity.

It may be dangerous to generalize, but one of the main reasons for the rapid expansion of the new religions, especially in the post-war period, has been that the older, more established sects of Buddhism and Shinto have become too formalized and have not, for the most part, carried out an educational program of the basic tenets of their religion among their members. In that respect, they may be like many Christian members here in Canada who observe the ceremonies but know very little about the Bible.

Central to the established Shinto and Buddhist sects has been the veneration of the dead. Although this has its value, the chanting of prayers for the dead often becomes the main pre-occupation of the priests. A good part of their work seems to be going from house to house to chant prayers on the anniversaries up to five years or more after a death. There often seems to be little time for anything else. One of the reasons I was attracted to the Sasaki father and son priests was that they did take time for teaching and for community service.

An interesting phenomenon in Japan is the fact that most weddings are performed in Shinto shrines and funeral services are usually in Buddhist temples. I have had the opportunity of attending both weddings and funerals and appreciating their ceremonies. It appears that some Japanese people are married in a Shinto shrine, buried in a Buddhist ceremony and also turn up occasionally for Christmas worship, trying, it would seem, to get all the bases covered.

SEICHO NO IE

Since over 95 percent of the people in Japan belong to faiths other than Christianity, almost all of our immediate neighbours were associated either with a Buddhist temple in town, the Nayoro Shinto shrine, or one of the new religions. One neighbour family was active in a new religion called Seicho No Ie "House of Growth." Our neighbours had regular meetings in their own home. We never attended any services but did visit them from time to time since their children and ours played together. I was interested in learning the background of Seicho No Ie. It is said to be the most eclectic of the new religions. The founder of Seicho No Ie was Masaharu Taniguchi who incorporated teachings from Buddhism, Christianity, psychology and Christian Science. He was especially fond of the Johannine writings of the Bible and published his own commentary of the Gospel of John. Physical and psychological health make up a central core of this religion and healing ministries are a large part of its appeal.

A monthly magazine entitled "Seicho-No-Ie" lays out its central teachings summed up in its "Proclamation of the Seven Rays of Light." Its teachings have many parallels with Christianity, including the belief that "Love is the best nourishment for Life and that prayer and words of love and praise are the creative Way of the Word, necessary to bring Love into manifestation."

Seicho No Ie is just one example of dozens of new religions which have proliferated since the 1930s.

SOKA GAKKAI

The fastest growing new religion has been the Soka Gakkai (Value Creation Society) This is an offshoot of Nichiren Buddhism and unlike other Japanese religions is dogmatic, intolerant and is active in proselytizing by sometimes devious means. It might be compared somewhat to present-day television evangelists. Although active in pre-war years it was suppressed during the war and has shown its spectacular growth in the post-war era under new leaders Josei Toda (until his death in 1958) and Daisaku Ikeda. By 1975 the Ministry of Education counted over 16 million as members of the Soka Gakkai, four times the size of its nearest rival, the Rissho Koseikai.

Soka Gakkai owes its success to its strict military-like structure and its methods of winning converts. The organizational structure is from household, to squad, to company, to district, to region, to headquarters, each with their defined area of responsibility. The main method of proselytizing is called "shakubuku" and involves the breaking down of resistance by determined arguments, extravagant promises and fearsome warnings. This is usually carried out in a team rather than by individuals. In the book, *Modern Japanese Religions*, Clark Offner writes:

> By promising them the world if they join and misfortune if they don't, Soka Gakkai has been especially successful with non-unionized workers in medium and small companies such as the Kyushu coal miners.

Spiritual healing through faith is an important part of its message. However, when a sickness does not respond to their healing practices, sick persons are often devastated by being told that their faith is not strong enough.

Soka Gakkai has had ambitions of gaining power politically. Founding a new political party called the "Komeito" they for a time, made spectacular gains in both the Upper and Lower

House elections for the Japanese Diet (Parliament). For a time there was considerable fear that if they gained a majority they might establish a dictatorial, fundamentalist type of government. However, this fear has been unfounded, for although they still have significant numbers in government, they have never been close to taking over the government.

RISSHO KOSEIKAI

One of the new religions for which I have a good deal of admiration is the Rissho Koseikai which means "Society for the Establishment of Righteousness and Fostering Fellowship." I had heard and read much about Rissho Koseikai for some time and became quite interested in some of its teachings, its educational methods and its work for world peace. In 1988 when I took a tour group to Japan I arranged a visit to their Great Sacred Hall (Daiseido) in Suginami Ward in Tokyo. This building, finished in 1964 at the cost of eleven million dollars, can accommodate thirty thousand worshippers at one time.

We were immediately impressed by the huge structure, built of pink tile and topped with a large dome. We were welcomed and shown around the seven storey building with its wide variety of facilities, ranging from a huge central worship hall, circled by three balconies where "hoza" groups can meet on the carpeted floor. The building also has a large cafeteria, reception hall, elevators and a magnificent German pipe organ. The focal point of the sanctuary is an impressive statue of a gold painted "Eternal Original Buddha."

We were shown a video depicting some of their many activities throughout Japan and of their work for peace in the world. We were privileged to meet the founder and leader Mr. Nikkyo Niwano, who is not a priest but a lay leader with a passion for peace, justice and ecumenical relations. He told us especially about his activities for world peace. He has been active overseas as a representative of a "Peace Delegation of Religious Leaders for Banning Atomic Weapons." He has also been active in the United Nations and had an audience with the Pope. I felt that he was truly an humble man with a love and compassion for all of humanity.

Nikkyo Niwano had a truly ecumenical dimension to his faith. In an article he wrote on, "A Buddhist Approach to Peace" he declares;

> The religious cooperation that I advocate does not stop at the shaking of hands by people of different religions but aims at reaching the stage where by studying in depth the true meaning of various religions, one can fathom the truth common to each religion and, by grasping this common truth, perceive oneness spontaneously.

I also have come to the understanding that every religion has a part of the truth, and that we need to work for mutual respect and understanding. An interchange of the truths we have discovered about life and religion can only lead to an enlargement of our own personal faith.

I was especially impressed by the fact that Rissho Koseikai has no priestly caste. All leaders - national officials, worship leaders, preachers, hoza leaders and theologians are lay people. Doctrine is based on the Lotus Sutra but is interpreted in modern simple terms by lay people for lay people. At every worship service the following readily understood Rissho Koseikai Creed is recited:

> We the members of Rissho Koseikai, under the leadership of our revered teacher, President Niwano, recognize the essential way of salvation in Buddhism and pledge our best efforts, in the spirit of Buddhist laymen, to perfect our character and realize in our lives the Bodhisstva Way. To this end, by improving in knowledge and practice of the faith, in personal discipline and in leading others, we will endeavour to realize a state of peace for the family, the community, the country, and the world.

The organization is centred in the Daiseido (Great Sacred Hall) to which members are expected to make frequent pilgrimages. Throughout Japan there are some 220 churches. All the local groups have trained lay leaders. Organization is formed in a pyramid structure with direct vertical lines of authority. This is a rather typical Japanese social structure.

What interested me most was their method of teaching and ministering through the "hoza." The hoza are small groups of twelve to fifteen members in which both teaching and the sharing of personal problems of group members take place. The purpose of the hoza is to apply Buddhist teaching to everyday problems. For instance, even when great crowds come to worship at the main worship hall, hundreds of small groups meet in circles, sitting on the carpeted floors in the balconies of the Great Hall. All the groups meet at the same time giving the sense of group solidarity. Even the children are welcomed and wander in and out at their leisure.

Each hoza is provided with a well trained lay leader who is both teacher and counsellor. Hoza sessions are geared toward solving members' actual problems, and often involve relating personal testimonies of how faith has affected one's life. In this respect they may resemble western group therapy sessions. There is an emotional acceptance on the part of the group and mutual support outside the group as well. A large proportion of those who attend these sessions are women and often the stories they tell have to do with family relationships. Both the leader and the group can share in finding solutions. Many of these solutions may be related to some of the teachings of the Buddhist faith, but these are dealt with not in the abstract but in relation to the specific problem at hand.

It is interesting to contrast Soka Gakkai and Rissho Koseikai. Both had their origins in Nichiren Buddhism, but have gone in two quite different directions. Whereas Soka Gakkai tends to be rigid, exclusive and aggressive, Rissho Koseikai is more flexible, ecumenical, and accommodating. Soka Gakkai does have a world outreach, but mostly in order to win converts, a program that in terms of winning followers all over the world has been quite successful. Rissho Koseikai has the wider perspective of working for peace in the world. Neither would seem to have a "social gospel" element in the sense of challenging the structures of society in order to make them more democratic. The aim of both Soka Gakkai and Rissho Koseikai is not to make strong individual personalities, but to help people to fit into society and to be happy in the process. The hoza has been described as "circles of harmony." One of its most important functions is to help people to feel at home in the society to which they belong.

Although the hoza approach may have factors like authoritarianism and didactic elements that would not fit well in western society, I think there is much that Christian churches could learn from their goals and procedures. Some of these we adapted in our "Three Love Schools" for young farmers at the Dohoku Centre. Although we let participants know that the Bible was the basis of much of our life and work it was never forced on anyone. Where the Bible was used in voluntary morning sessions the studies were always related to some of the personal, social or national issues that we were discussing.

The hoza demonstrates the effectiveness of using trained lay leaders for both teaching and counselling. This has been one of my own visions for new life within the church. It was one of the reasons that I put a good deal of effort during my time on the staff of the Prairie Christian Training Centre, into training lay leadership. During my final year on staff I helped to develop a lay training course called "Laity in Action" based on some of the principles learned from the Rissho Koseikai model. Participants developed a sense of their own worth and their own particular ministry in church and society, and found joy and self-fulfilment in their new-found tasks.

DEVELOPING INTERFAITH DIALOGUE IN CANADA

Because of meaningful encounters with people of other faiths in Japan, when I came back to live in Canada I was anxious to promote interfaith dialogue and deeper mutual understanding among different faith groups. This opportunity came when I served on the staff of the Prairie Christian Training Centre from 1982 to 1988.

One of the programs I helped to develop was a yearly series of weekend events on the mission of the church in Canada and the world. For many of these I had the assistance of the Rev. Lois Wilson, who at that time was Director of the Ecumenical

Forum in Toronto and who later became the first woman Moderator of the United Church of Canada. One of these events was "Dialoguing with People of Other Faiths." I brought together leaders in the Jewish, Muslim, Bahai and Christian faiths from Regina. One of the things that these four faiths had in common was that they all claimed Abraham as a founding father.

Representatives of each faith group shared what was most meaningful to them in their faith. We discussed our commonalities and differences and discussed ways in which we could work together more effectively. We decided that one of the best ways was not getting bogged down in differences but in working to get to know people from other faith traditions. We also put as one of our goals that of cooperating in projects that would bring greater social justice to society and peace in the world.

My next opportunity for interfaith dialogue came after I left the Prairie Christian Training Centre in 1988 and was serving for a four-month period as an interim Director of the Ecumenical Forum in Toronto. One of the mandates of the Forum was to facilitate inter-faith dialogue. As part of our role for carrying out this mandate we were asked to help to organize a North American event in Toronto on Muslim/Christian Relations. Prominent Muslims and Christians from the United States and Canada gathered for a weekend in Toronto. One of the interesting features of this event was that a Christian with a background in Muslim studies presented the Muslim faith as he understood it and a Muslim with a knowledge of the Christian faith presented his understanding of Christianity. This led into a lively and fruitful discussion. Another interesting dialogue was on the issue of Muslim/Christian weddings. In order to observe their daily times of prayer the Muslims withdrew to another room for their devotions. This was a demonstration of the important place of prayer in the Muslim faith.

After leaving the staff of the Ecumenical Forum I was asked to continue as the editor of a Forum periodical called the "Fish Eye Lens." In the June 1989 edition on "Interfaith Perspectives on Peace" I included statements from Christian, Islamic, Buddhist, Jewish, Bahai and Marxist representatives. Each of these reveal a firm commitment to peace arising out of their beliefs. For instance, Mrs. Sugi Yamamoto, Director of the All Japan Buddhist Women's Association says:

> Our talk of peace must always include justice. The starving person and the dying child, whether caught in drought, war or other disaster, cannot be concerned with peace, but only with the struggle to survive.

Dr. Inamullah Khan of the World Muslim Conference from Pakistan reports:

> Islam stands for peace: peace for all, peace without discrimination; peace on the basis of justice.

Udo Schaefer of the Bahai Faith declares:

> Peace and justice will be the fruit of the spiritual rebirth of mankind, a complete change in the consciousness of the new man, a new order and a labourious process of construction.

Y. Zhilin, from Russia says:

> Peace is not just the absence of war. Its preservation presupposes the creation of an all-embracing system of international security. It presupposes universal and tireless efforts, purposeful advancement towards real disarmament, reducing political confrontation, negotiated settlement of disputes and development of international cooperation in all fields.

Each faith perspective enlarges our vision of peace and pushes us toward joint actions for a more peaceful and just society. Why should we persist in taking action on issues of justice and peace by ourselves, when we could do them so much more effectively by doing them together with people of other faith backgrounds?

NATIVE SPIRITUALITY

While on the staff of the Prairie Christian Training Centre I had the privilege of being associated with the work of the Dr. Jesse Saulteaux Centre for the training of native pastors for native churches in Saskatchewan and Manitoba. The Director, Rev. Alf Dumont from time to time asked the staff of the P.C.T.C. to assist in the leadership of some of the courses. This association gave me the opportunity to understand a unique type of training. It was an on-the-job training in which the students served in native churches on weekends and came to the Centre for training three days a week. In his teaching Alf developed a blend of Christian faith and native spirituality. In addition to learning Christian ceremonies the students participated in sweat lodges and listened to teachings of traditional native elders.

Since coming to Peterborough I have had many contacts with people from the nearby Curve Lake Reserve. Merritt Taylor, a traditional native elder, has assisted in leading interfaith services, opening with the native sweet grass ceremony. "Sweet grass" is a grass that gives off a pungent odour when burned. As smoke arises from the sweet grass it is carried around a circle and the participants cup the smoke in their hands and cover their head with the smoke as a cleansing ceremony. The native elder then says a prayer, first in the Ojibway language and then in English, thanking the Creator for the beauties of nature and the gift of life.

Merritt also teaches the Ojibway language and native culture in the public schools of Lakefield. My two grand-daughters, who live in Lakefield, have taken his classes and enjoyed them tremendously. I have also listened to his talks on native spirituality and have found much of worth for my own faith in the native understanding of the earth and love and respect for all its creatures. I am also impressed by his daily discipline of rising before sunrise for a period of meditation.

I have also participated in a sweat lodge ceremony led by native elder and Laurentian University Professor, Herb Nabigon. This ceremony takes place in a tightly enclosed tent with a pit in the centre containing hot stones on which water is poured to make steam. The participants sit in a circle in complete darkness, as the leader gives a meditation and prayer, and invites anyone who wishes to share any of their joys and burdens. This ceremony provides a cleansing of body, mind and spirit and can often lead to a new understanding of the self and the finding of new directions in life. I believe that native spirituality and teachings like the ones I have mentioned have much to add to our Christian teachings and practices.

All of the opportunities that I have had of getting to know personally people of other faiths and studying other religions have enlarged my vision of the truths found in all religions. My senses have been sharpened to see both the positives and negatives of my own faith and of other religions. For instance, most of the religions including Christianity and Judaism, are exceedingly patriarchal. Too many rely on charismatic individuals, rather than giving lay leaders important roles. Although a few of the Japanese new religions have had women founders, almost all are led by males. Women in the churches are only recently being accepted as "clergy" and in some denominations are still excluded. However, in Christianity and in many of the world religions, in spite of the negative aspects, there are streams of authenticity that we cannot ignore. There is a growing spirituality that transcends the structures and doctrines.

I have seen more clearly than ever that if we are to have success in tackling the immense issues of peace and injustice in our world we can never do it alone, but must unite our efforts on a world-wide scale. These have been some of the insights I have gained from other religions and ways of life on my own journey of faith.

COMMUNITIES OF FAITH

I have been fortunate that much of the time on my journey of faith I have had the support of intimate faith communities which have helped to clear my vision and strengthen my faith.

After coming to Peterborough I have been participating in an early Friday morning interchurch, interfaith community for meditation, joint Bible study and in-depth sharing. This group, that is made up of a wide variety of people involved in many aspects of work in church and community, provides me spiritual sustenance at a deeper level than that provided by more formal worship services. This group began about fifteen years ago as a support group of Catholic lay people involved in providing housing for single mothers with small children. The group was expanded to include people from Anglican, United, Presbyterian, Unitarian, Buddhist and others who don't identify themselves with any specific religion.

My experience has been that these small group communities have given me strength and support in facing daily challenges. They have helped to overcome periods of loneliness and frustration when the road got rough.

A NEW LOVING PARTNERSHIP

The person who introduced me to the Friday morning interfaith community immediately after our marriage on November 19, 1994 was my new partner, Sheila. The story of our meeting and friendship is an interesting happenstance.

When Doreen and I were preparing to retire and leave the Prairie Christian Training Centre, Hazel Jardine, a member of the Fort Qu'Appelle Ploughshares peace group, attended a national conference of Project Ploughshares in Waterloo. Her roommate at Conrad Grebel College was Sheila Nabigon. Hazel mentioned that Doreen and I were retiring and planning to move to Ontario to be closer to our two children Dennis and Susan and their families. On her return to Peterborough Sheila immediately wrote a letter to Doreen and myself saying, "Come to Peterborough and join our Ploughshares group. We need new members. We would welcome you with open arms." We returned to Ontario in early July and lived first in Toronto before settling in Lakefield, near Peterborough.

We got in touch with Sheila and found out the time and place for the next Ploughshares meeting. Immediately we had a new group of friends, and were especially happy to meet Sheila who had extended us that warm invitation. Sheila became a close friend of both Doreen and myself.

After Doreen's death I was devastated and very lonely. The members of Kawartha Ploughshares were a strong support group. Over a two year period the friendship between Sheila and I deepened. I wondered for a time if there was too much difference in our ages to consider marriage, but we finally decided that since we had so much in common in our concerns for peace, justice and international relations that age should not be a barrier. The fact that she was Roman Catholic and I a Protestant did not really concern us since both of us were ecumenical in our outlooks. In the spring of 1994 we made a commitment, but agreed to test it out during the summer when Sheila was going to Jamaica on a Jamaican Self Help summer project and I to Japan to visit my family. On our return we set a date for our wedding, which took place November 19th in the Lakefield United Church with the Rev. George Addison as the presiding minister. There were about 120 guests for a gourmet pot-luck supper followed by square dancing with Ken Ramsden's band. The wedding was a really joyous occasion.

In our wedding invitation we requested that there be no wedding gifts, since with two households we had more than enough to furnish our home. We suggested that if anyone wished to give a gift they could make a contribution to Project Ploughshares, the Canadian Catholic Organization for Development and Peace (CCODP) or Jamaican Self Help.

Sheila and I have had a truly happy time together. Both of us are involved in community projects, some together and some separately. Kawartha Ploughshares has been a continuing commitment for both of us. For a time I was Co-Chair and she was Secretary. We have been involved in several special campaigns sponsored by Kawartha Ploughshares: two forums with Peterborough City Council on the abolition of nuclear weapons; a campaign to eliminate landmines; a multi-media presentation on the devastation caused by landmines that was presented at several churches and at the Lakefield High School for Remembrance Day. We also attended the world conference on the abolition of landmines in Ottawa in 1999. Kawartha Ploughshares has had an ongoing campaign against the Gulf War and the sanctions against the people of Iraq in which over a million people have died. We have helped to produce pamphlets and written many letters to government leaders and to newspapers on this issue. In 1997 Sheila and I both received a peace medallion from the Peterborough YMCA for our work for peace in Peterborough and around the world.

In June of 2001 Sheila was awarded a Community Betterment Award from the City of Peterborough for her "outstanding contribution to the community."

Sheila has been very active in support of refugees and immigrants. She cooperated with the New Canadian Centre in setting up a monthly pot-luck supper at which newcomers to Canada could have fellowship with each other and with long time Canadians. This filled a real need. Sometimes there were as many as fifteen different nationalities. In the fall of 2001 Sheila was honoured for her service to new Canadians by a citation from the New Canadian Centre.

I have been Co-chair of the Peterborough Coalition for Social Justice and Sheila was the CCODP representative on the planning committee. We have both been involved in the interchurch Ten Days for Global Justice Programme. In 2001 this national programme was re-organized into KAIROS - Canadian Ecumenical Justice Initiatives. We have been a part of the reorganization and members of the continuing committee. Sheila was for several years the Co-ordinator of the Peterborough Diocese of the CCODP until she was elected to the National CCODP Council which involves frequent trips to Montreal. Through her CCODP connection Sheila was chosen as one of the delegates from the Canadian Council of Churches to the Anti-Racism Conference in Durban, South Africa in the summer of 2001. On her return she shared her experience with many church and community groups.

Once a month for several years we hosted a meeting of the Affirm United support group for gay and lesbian Christians in our home, until the group decided to have monthly worship services in the St. Andrew's United Church, in which we also participate.

Both of us enjoy our new extended families. Clem and Alana Nabigon have become step-son and step-daughter for me, and Dennis, Peter and Susan have become family for Sheila.

She also inherited nine grandchildren who call her "grandma Sheila."

Sheila and I have both found a new fulfilment in our love and lives together and give thanks that we found each other and can work together so compatibly.

Floyd and Sheila

12

ONGOING CHALLENGES TO FAITH

As I look back over my life in Japan and my faith journey, I find there are several themes that have dominated my life and informed my faith. These have been a growing revelation of new facets of my faith. I never had, and do not now have a sense of having arrived. There is so much more to learn and experience in my faith journey. The road ahead is always exciting and filled with new challenges and expectations.

The traumatic event of the destruction of the World Trade Centre in New York and the Pentagon in Washington on September 11th, 2001 has been a major setback for the peace and justice movement, and a new challenge for people of faith. U.S. President George Bush's call for a "war on terrorism" and his statement that those who are not for us, are for the enemy has opened up the possibility of continuous warfare for years to come. In my opinion, the oil magnates and arms manufacturers, now entrenched in the White House, look upon the war on terrorism as an opportunity to expand the military and to take over control of the oil resources of the world. After Afghanistan, they targeted Iraq, a country that has already suffered 12 years of sanctions and air raids with over one million casualties.

Peace, in the Bible, is a multi-faceted word. In his letter to the Philippians (Chapter 4, Verse 7), Paul speaks of "the peace which is far beyond human understanding." We can't really grasp all its dimensions. Peace was the life passion of many of the leaders and guides whom I respected most: Edis Fairbairn, Jim Finlay, and Toyohiko Kagawa. Fairbairn and Finlay both put their careers on the line in their opposition to World War II. Jim Finlay by his actions showed us that in addition to being opposed to war we must also become involved in serving the victims of war. Toyohiko Kagawa endured prison and torture for conscience sake, but he also insisted that simply being opposed to war would not in itself solve the issues of war and peace. Unless the economic issues underlying war are dealt with, we will fail in trying to build a peaceful world. One of the ways in which he saw the economic system being reformed was through a cooperative movement based on love rather than individual gain. For this reason, he put much of his life's effort into promoting the cooperative movement among farmers, labourers, consumers, and through credit unions. He also helped to found the Socialist Party in Japan. Through his actions Kagawa shows that in order to work for peace we will also have to be involved in issues of both economics and politics.

After the planes flew into the twin towers of the World Trade Centre in New York, it was reported that a little girl asked her mother, "Why do they hate us?" That is perhaps the most pertinent question we should be asking. It was no coincidence that the terrorists chose the Trade Centre as their prime target. With the growing economic gap between the north and the south and the rampant exploitation of Third World nations by mostly U.S. based multinational corporations, it is not surprising that those exploited have come to hate the rich nations of the North. Hate begets terrorism and terrorism feeds on terrorism. The terrorism of the dissidents led to an even more vicious terrorist war in Afghanistan, in 2001, by the U.S. and compliant countries like the United Kingdom and Canada.

We recognize the trauma faced by the families of the victims of the attack on the World Trade Centre, but why can't we also feel the pain of the Afghani families who have lost loved ones? Aren't these military actions also acts of terrorism?

As this book is being prepared for publication at the end of May 2003 the U.S., Britain, and several other countries have just begun the occupation of Iraq. It has already been proven that the propaganda about terrorism and weapons of mass destruction used to justify the invasion were all equally spurious.

The threat of war galvanized a global peace movement with millions around the world joining in protest rallies and actions. A coalition of peace activists in Peterborough and district were a part of this action with over one hundred gathering every Saturday afternoon for rallies that included the singing of anti-war songs, signing petitions and writing letters to the government of Canada demanding that it not get involved in a war against the people of Iraq. This did have the effect of keeping Canada out of direct involvement in the war in spite of tremendous pressure from U.S. government leaders.

The Kawartha Ploughshares peace group was one of the main leaders of this coalition. This was a culmination of over three years of weekly vigils in front of the local Federal Member of Parliament's office protesting the sanctions that had caused the deaths of over one and a half million Iraqis. M.P. Peter Adams was supportive to the extent that he continued to convey our message to Parliament.

Although leaders of mainline churches did make strong statements and lobbied the government against the war, unfortunately the same could not be said of many local ministers or congregations. Many certainly prayed for peace but seemed to fear alienating parts of the congregation who held a pro-war stance. Only a few of the ministers joined the protests and vigils. There is still a lot of peace education needed to demonstrate that waging war never brings peace. We must work much harder at developing the non-violent strategies that can lead to peace. Fairbairn, Finlay and Kagawa still have much to teach us. True security can be achieved only when all people are assured of their rights and basic needs.

JUSTICE

Without justice there is no peace. The pursuit of justice is a major theme of the Bible, exemplified by the words of the prophet Micah (Verse 6, Chapter 8); "What does God require of you but to do justice, and to love kindness, and to walk humbly with your God."

For me the awakening to the injustice of our society struck me most vividly, when I saw the cruel and unjust treatment of Japanese Canadians at the outbreak of World War II. Following the lead of Jim Finlay I threw myself into the support of fellow Canadians, who had been put in prison camps just because of their race.

The experience of working with Japanese Canadians who were discriminated against sharpened my sensitivity to racism and persecution of other nationalities. Martin Luther King Jr. and James Cone introduced me to the struggle for justice of black Americans. Toshimitsu Miyajima in his book, *Land Of Elms*, gave me a better understanding of the persecution of the Ainu in Hokkaido by the Japanese. Their insights prepared me to fight against racism of every kind, in whatever country human beings were denigrated.

In July 2002, Matthew Coon Come, the National Chief of the Assembly of First Nations, was shown on television tearing up a copy of the federal government's proposal for a "First Nations Governance Act." The government had ignored the 1996 comprehensive report of the Royal Commission on Aboriginal Peoples, that had spoken of the inherent right of self government, the right that allows First Nations to make laws on their own initiative with regard to internal matters, without the approval of the federal government. It is not surprising that Matthew Coon Come and other First Nations Chiefs are infuriated by the action of the federal government.

The Assembly of First Nations called upon all Canadians who believe in our values of diversity and social justice to reject this Act. This government proposal is another example of a blatant injustice that churches in Canada need to vehemently oppose, while lending their full support to aboriginal peoples in their struggle for the full recognition of native rights. Without justice, there can be no peace between us who have adopted Canada as our homeland and with the First Nations People of Canada.

LOVE

Without love there can be neither justice nor peace. Love must undergird all our efforts for peace and justice in the world. Love is the pre-eminent theme of the Bible. Love also undergirded the lives and work of my mentors both in Canada and Japan. Toyohiko Kagawa in a book entitled, *Love the Law of Life*, identifies love as "life's motive power." His own life exhibited love's motivation in his willingness to live in the slums of Kobe and share his meagre livelihood with street people.

In the Gospel of Matthew (Chapter 5, Verses 33 & 34), Jesus showed us the close connection between love and peace when he said "Love your enemies and pray for those who persecute you, so that you may become children of your Father in heaven." To me, "God is Love" and "Love is God" is more than a tautology. It delineates the way in which God becomes known. God can never be defined; only through acts of love can the love of God be exemplified. Many of my associates in Japan exhibited this kind of self giving love. I only need to recall the life and death of Alfred Stone, the self giving service of Mitsuko Hosoumi in the Shibetsu and Wassamu churches, and the self effacing ministries of Mrs. Shiomi, the lay woman in the Nayoro church, to recognize love in action, reflections of the nature and being of God. Our work for peace and justice in the world must always be undergirded by love for all of God's people.

THE ROLE OF THE BIBLE

The Bible has always been central in my faith, but I have also felt a great ambivalence toward the Bible. I give thanks that early in my life Edis Fairbairn and Northrop Frye freed me from a literalist approach to the Biblical text. They helped me see that there is much in the Bible which must be discounted, that it often reflects the mores and prejudices of the times in which the various narratives were written. Much of it is patriarchal, sexist and monarchical. Parts of the Old Testament justify revenge and glorify war. Parts of the New Testament can be interpreted as anti-Semitic. However, throughout the Bible there are recurring central themes of love, justice and peace, that give the Biblical message an authenticity that cannot be discounted.

Northrop Frye helped me to get beyond the literal text by means of interpretation through myth and metaphor. As the little Student Christian Movement study group, of which I was a member, sat in his office and traced the recurring myths and metaphors in the Bible, we began to see it more as poetry than prose. We recognized it as a great book of literature, but at the same time more than great literature. The myths and metaphors of Scripture became words that we could live by. They not only worked for us but expanded our horizons and led us to want to pass the insights on to others.

I have found my faith sustenance mostly in the prophets, the Gospels and some of the Psalms. What we can know of the person of Jesus and his teachings, points to a way of life worth imitating. His response to the evil in the world and his willingness to suffer under persecution rather than seek revenge is a pattern that, though hard to follow, is certainly a goal for which I strive. I cannot accept the Biblical claim of Jesus as the only "son of God" or as "the saviour of the world." Jesus himself referred to himself mostly as "son of man." Jesus has the expectation that all of us can be sons and daughters of God. He says that God's spirit is evident in human interactions of mercy, compassion, forgiveness, sharing, working for justice, and working for peace. When we do these things, God's spirit is in us. He also says that all people, not just Christians, are people through whom the Spirit of God works. Wherever love, joy, justice and peace are evident, there God is.

Frye says that the Gospels give us the life of Jesus in the form of myth, not to be taken literally, but "as a myth to live by." For that reason we can retain the central messages of the stories of Jesus' birth and resurrection. These "mythical" stories point us to the possibility of our re-birth as we take on new life directions, and as we learn to face death with tranquillity, knowing that to the extent we have experienced a God of love, we have nothing to fear, whatever our future holds.

THE IRRELEVANCE OF THE CHURCHES

Although many churches are very good at ministering to their own members and in creating a fellowship of the initiated, for the most part, the church has become almost irrelevant in terms of its impact on the world. It is as if people of the church are happy living within the cocoon of the church and want to be shielded from the dangers and stresses of the world around them. However, the question we need to ask ourselves is this:

is ministering to the faithful, the primary mission to which the Gospels call us?

J. C. Hoekendijk awakened me to the fact that Church-centric missionary thinking revolves around an illegitimate centre. On the contrary, the world and the Kingdom should be at the centre of our theology of mission. This was the theology and practice of Toyohiko Kagawa in the Kingdom of God Movement, seeking to minister to the practical needs of almost every sector of Japanese society. This was also the advice of Toshi Kimata when he referred to most Japanese churches as being no more than "cut-flowers decorating their respective communities as accessories of urban modern life." He added that churches could not succeed unless they were intimately rooted in the every-day life of their communities. Following Kimata's advice, the Dohoku Centre developed an outreach to the community, beyond the borders of the churches, especially in its work with rural youth.

On coming back to Canada, I discovered that most of the churches were caught in the same self-serving trap, ministering primarily to their own needs and wants, without regard to the crying needs of the society around them or of the issues of world poverty and war. Two examples spring to mind, one concerning community, and the other of an international nature.

Within the Peterborough Presbytery of the United Church, a very active Outreach Committee sought to identify several of the most urgent needs of local communities. They identified three priority needs to which they felt churches should be alerted for action. They were, the dire shortage of affordable housing, the needs of the mentally ill, and the restorative justice approach to the criminal justice system. Community Outreach Forums were planned for various parts of the Presbytery, grouping together three or four area churches for each forum. However, although the forums had knowledgeable presenters for each topic, and excellent discussion periods, the attendance was very poor. Although all the issues being discussed were very relevant to all the communities, it seemed that the church members were not prepared to hear about the issues, let alone to do anything about them.

The second, international example has to do with the effect of the repressive trade sanctions against the people of Iraq. The Division of World Outreach Committee of the United Church, of which I was a vocal member, presented a resolution to the annual meeting of the Bay of Quinte Conference, consisting of over 500 delegates from churches in eastern Ontario, asking the Canadian Government to use its influence to get the U.N. sanctions against the people of Iraq lifted. The resolution was not given priority and for lack of time was deferred to the Executive for later consideration. When the Executive met they decided that they couldn't make a decision because of lack of information. It took another year before the resolution was again considered by the full Conference and was finally passed. However, although the resolution was sent to the Federal Government and to local churches, I did not hear of any local church that took up the issue of lifting sanctions as a priority.

During his three years as Moderator of the United Church the Rev. Bill Phipps made a valiant effort to try to awaken the church to its responsibility for dealing with issues of the growing economic gap, between the rich and poor in Canada and globally. Speaking out boldly, in travels to churches across Canada he urged churches to organize "Moral Economy" workshops in their communities. I do not know what response the challenge to study the issues received across Canada, but only one church in the Peterborough Presbytery held a Moral Economy Workshop. It saddens me that most churches are neglecting the issues of justice, peace and love which are so central to the Biblical message.

THE CHURCH AS INSTITUTION OR COMMUNITIES ON A JOURNEY?

I have always had difficulty accepting the church as an institution. One reason I hesitated to become a minister of the church, was because I was painfully aware of the hypocrisy of the institutional church. Because of their failure to take a stand against World War II, Edis Fairbairn accused all Churches of being "apostate." He defined "apostate" as being off one's base, acting

Ongoing Challenges to Faith

not in accordance with one's proper standards. In his book, *Apostate Christendom*, he states:

> The original impulse of the early Christian community manifested itself instinctively in two specific protests, against the dominance of money and against the practice of war. Modern Christendom has allowed itself to become willingly chained to the chariots of Mars and Mammon.

Although some people within the church still speak out against Canada's military build up and participation in war, the church as a whole is regrettably silent. When Christians speak out against the economic system and seek to bring about changes, many churches fail to support the protest, saying that economic issues are "too political." Fairbairn's description of institutional churches as apostate has unfortunately been borne out in my own experience. Most of the churches are "off base."

My study of the role of the laity has also had an important influence on my thinking. I have been inspired by the writings of Kanzo Uchimura, the founder of the "mukyokai" non-church movement in Japan. Uchimura speaks out strongly for:

> a church free from all ecclesiasticism - a fellowship, not an institution - a free communion of souls, not a system or an organization - a churchless Christianity, calling no man bishop or pastor save Jesus Christ.

His ideal of a "churchless Christianity" may be difficult to realize. There will always be a need for leaders, but his call for ridding the church of "ecclesiasticism" remains valid. The question is what kind of leadership do we really want? Do we really need a special "order of ministry"? Shouldn't all Christians have a ministry and the main function of the church be to help each Christian identify and implement his or her ministry? What place is there for clerical collars, ecclesiastical robes, and the title of Reverend? Do these not just set up barriers between ("priestly" and "lay") orders within the church? Should we not rather expect our leaders to exemplify the gifts of the Holy Spirit, especially those of love and humility?

Another place in which inequalities in most denominations become evident is in the bureaucracy of national church organizations. For instance, the United Church has just gone through a massive restructuring process (2000-2001). Regrettably, it has been restructured according to a corporate model, with a managerial class and worker/staff organization, with significant differences in compensation.

Some church and community organizations, including the staff of the Prairie Christian Training Centre, have experimented with a collective model. I admit that in a society that has been so accustomed to the corporate model the ideal of the collective model may be hard to maintain, but if a church is to be really a community of equals, should we not be striving for church structures that correspond to our ideals?

The fact is that many former church members who have become so disillusioned with the church have left it altogether. Others, like myself, even though dissatisfied, still hang in, trying to bring about change from within, but feeling more and more like exiles, who don't really belong. However, though many have left the institutional church, this does not mean that they have given up the search for spirituality and a new meaning in life. Where can we go, to find satisfaction and new directions?

In order to find a new path it is necessary to critique the church structures and beliefs of the past, so that we can see more clearly what can safely be discarded and what should be preserved.

Many people are looking for final and definitive answers. That is one reason some are attracted to fundamentalist churches. These churches, have a sort of formula religion, that offers certain salvation, if one just believes a certain set of dogmas, and lives out a certain set of values. These religions, which promise heaven or nirvana at the end of life, offer a sort of "pie in the sky by and by" faith.

In my own experience and studies I do not believe, that we can ever live with certainty. We must always keep seeking and searching, changing and growing. If we try to stand still, we stagnate. We must say to ourselves and others, "This is where I am now in my faith journey, and I must act with the knowledge I have now, knowing that if I make mistakes, I will be prepared to admit errors and go on to gain new insights."

In my search for meaning I have found considerable assistance from the writings of Dairmuid O'Murchu, who now works as a counsellor and social psychologist in England. In his book, *Religion in Exile*, he writes of his growing disillusionment with the institutional church and his search for new forms of spirituality, both within the Christian tradition and outside. He points to the distinction between religion and spirituality, having met people from many cultures and social classes, who did not have a particular religion, but whose lives are clearly touched by a sense of the divine.

O'Murchu's main argument regarding, not only the Christian religion, but most of the world's religions, is that their fatal flaw, has been their dependence on patriarchy. He sees that we must go beyond patriarchy, by recognizing ourselves as spiritual beings, belonging in a spiritualized universe. This is the basis for Creation Spirituality, that looks upon God as Creator and on ourselves as co-creators with God. This sense of the spirit of God living and working within each, releases us from dependency on inspired teachers or patriarchs. It is soul freeing, to discover that ultimate truth, resides not in teachers or politicians or in clergy but within our own hearts. This may be very frightening for many, since it puts a greater responsibility on a person's shoulders in the search for truth, but is also a risk that must be taken if our faith is to remain relevant.

The journey of discovery, as O'Murchu describes it helps us to reclaim our affiliation with creation, our essential nature as a relational species; and our faith in the co-creative power of God. If we understand God having a relationship with the human species from the earliest time that there were human beings upon the earth, it follows that the real incarnation, God with us, occurs at that time, and that there is no need to think theologically about God as only being incarnate in Jesus. The whole myth of God Incarnate in Jesus has led to some fantastic theological speculations, such as God in three persons, and the role of Jesus as a redemptive sacrifice to take away the sin of the world.

The rejection of the doctrine of the Incarnation of God in Jesus does not prevent us from seeing in Jesus' life and death a unique revelation of God's love that can be a pattern for our own lives. A contemporary theologian, John Dominic Crossan, suggests that the death of Jesus should be regarded primarily as a political event incurred by the strong prophetic stance that Jesus adopted on behalf of humanity. Viewing Jesus' death in this light, we are challenged to follow Jesus in his prophetic mission, even if we too have to give up our lives. This interpretation has a strong appeal to me as I struggle to discover the place that Jesus should have in my faith and life.

When we examine the Gospels to find what was central in the teachings of Jesus we find that the heart and core of Jesus' vision is in the Basileia that has been translated as the Kingdom of God or the Reign of God or as O'Murchu prefers to call it, the "Kindom of God." I much prefer O'Murchu's translation since it avoids the monarchist, kingly overtones and puts the emphasis on the community of faith.

As an indication of the importance to Jesus of the Kindom of God, this phrase occurs 140 times in the four Gospels. It is hard to summarize all that Jesus was trying to impart through his parables and teachings about the Kindom, but essentially I see in them a challenge to accept full responsibility for the process of transformation, initiated in and through Jesus, and to commit ourselves to building a world order marked by building a kindom of right relationships based on justice, love and peace. Certainly, in the lives and mission of Edis Fairbairn, Jim Finlay and Toyohiko Kagawa the message of the Kindom was pivotal and they expressed its centrality in the witness of their own lives for justice love and peace.

PUTTING KINDOM THEOLOGY INTO PRACTICE
Since my retirement in Peterborough I have deliberately sought to put most of my volunteer service energy into the community rather than into church related projects. I saw this as an obligation if I were to carry out a theology of mission that regards the

world and not the church as the centre of Jesus' mission. What volunteer work I did in the church, through participation in the World Outreach Committee and Ten Days for Global Justice, was with the purpose of trying to make the church as a whole more aware of its mission to the world. However, I often felt as if this message was falling on deaf ears.

Shortly after I moved to the Peterborough area, Dean Shewring, who was at that time President of the Peterborough and District Labour Council, organized a series of noon-hour meetings during 1991-1992 aimed at getting the Labour Council more aware of and involved in issues facing the whole community. I attended these gatherings and suggested that for one of the meetings in 1992 we invite Mary Ann O'Connor, of the Ontario Coalition for Social Justice, as a special speaker. She spoke of the need for local social justice coalitions to coordinate social justice concerns. As a result of this proposal a community forum with the aim of working towards a Peterborough Coalition for Social Justice was planned.

This forum, that included representatives of a wide variety of community organizations, agreed to form a social justice coalition and identified social justice priorities of the group. I was elected Co-chair, with Kate Eichkorn, a Trent University, Women's Studies student as a the other Co-chair. Later Co-chairs were Directors of the Ontario Public Interest Research Group (OPIRG), Jill Ritchie and Marnie Eves. The connection with OPIRG was important since it was the student social action group for Trent University. This helped to tie social action in the city with social action on the campus. The steering committee drew up a mission statement that stated:

> The Peterborough Coalition for Social Justice is a broadly-based social action group committed to working towards justice and equality in our community. It is dedicated to advocating social and economic policies that lead to full employment and adequate social welfare programs. It is also committed to working towards quality education, universal access to

health care, enhanced seniors' pensions, environmental protection and equality for women.

The Coalition's first major action was the preparation of street theatre opposing the North American Free Trade Agreement (NAFTA), for presentation, first at a park in Peterborough and then at a national rally in Ottawa. Several busloads of people from the Coalition, the Peterborough Labour Council and other community organizations participated in the Ottawa rally.

The Coalition was co-sponsor, along with the Peterborough and District Labour Council, of the June 24th, 1996 Community Day of Action against the policies of the Ontario Government that were destroying the social safety net, downgrading education and denigrating the work of the labour unions. Several thousand people attended an outdoor rally.

Over the years the Coalition sponsored a wide variety of public meetings and community actions. Just to mention a few: In the fall of 1997, before the Peterborough City municipal election, an event was held to mark the International Day for the Eradication of Poverty at which the Coalition hosted a free lunch for people experiencing poverty and also invited candidates for municipal office to attend. During this meal, a hard-hitting drama about the maldistribution of wealth was presented, followed by an opportunity for dialogue with the politicians. Sylvia Sutherland, who became Mayor at that time, said afterwards that this event had changed her priorities for her term of office.

In January of 1998 the Coalition conducted a day long "teach-in" on the Multilateral Agreement on Investment (MAI) with Tony Clarke as the theme speaker. The Coalition also led yearly forums on Alternative Budgets to coincide with the presentations of both Federal and Provincial Budgets.

The Coalition has also given active support to public events sponsored by other community organizations, for example by the Peterborough Social Planning Council in its actions against child poverty , and a "Public Forum on Education Cuts" sponsored by "Education for Action Today." Members of the Coalition have also written many "Letters to the Editor" of local newspapers on current issues. The Coalition has been most successful in its goal of mobilizing a wide variety of community organizations for joint action on issues that affect us all.

For five years I served on the board of the Kawartha World Issues Centre, that does public education on world issues in schools, the university and in the community. I also served for five years on the Board of the Peterborough Social Planning Council, through the Council becoming involved in Committees dealing with food security and the lack of affordable housing.

Although I was not looking for approbation from the community, the volunteer activities I undertook within the community were not without recognition. In June of 2000 I was presented with an Award of Merit as the Volunteer of the Year by the City of Peterborough. In 2001 I was honoured with a plaque from the Peterborough and District Labour Council for Community Service. In June 2002 I was inducted into the Pathway of Fame as a "Community Samaritan" with my name inscribed on a marker in a walkway in Del Crary Park. At this last award, I remarked that I felt that in the community organizations in which I had served, I had been able to get a lot more out of them than I was able to put into them. I urged others to get involved and get the satisfaction that came from participation in social justice issues that affect us all.

BATTLING CANCER

On October 5, 1999 following a routine chest x-ray, lesions on my lung were discovered. After a biopsy these were identified as Non-Hodgkins, mantle cell lymphoma. Mantle cell is considered to be a low grade lymphoma, slow in growing but almost impossible to eradicate.

This information came as a great shock to Sheila and myself. For the first time I thought seriously about my own mortality, however I did not panic. Both Sheila and I determined to fight the cancer with every means at our disposal. We got information on alternative therapies with diets that increased general health and strengthened the immune system. My doctor brother, Maurice, sent us a great deal of useful information.

During the next two and one-half years I went through a course of low-dose chemotherapy treatments in 2000, followed by infusion of a new chemotherapy drug, Rituxin in the spring of 2001. These had some positive effects but did not eliminate the lymphoma. In the winter of 2002, a series of radiation treatments greatly relieved breathing difficulties. I have also had oxygen therapy.

What has been my psychological and spiritual response throughout this ordeal? Psychologically I have felt a great deal of frustration at not being able to do many of the things I had normally been able to do. This showed up when I wanted to put in a big garden. I found that I could do none of the heavy work. With the help of a high school student we were able to get the garden planted. Sheila also did a lot more work than formerly, especially in the flower garden. It concerns me that I haven't been able to do my share of the work around the house and this has put a greater burden on Sheila. I am very appreciative of the tremendous support Sheila has given me. I am also grateful for the love and support of my family and so many people in the community. Presently, in March of 2003, my oncologist says the lymphoma seems to be spreading very slowly, but he gave no prognosis. We continue to battle against the cancer but have no assurance that we can hold it in abeyance. However, we do not give up hope.

Spiritually I think that I am prepared for whatever comes. I do not fear death, though I want to go on living as long as I can. There is so much more to do in the community and in the world, working for peace. I have found a purpose in working to finish *Beyond Churchianity*. If it can be of any use in strengthening the faith and the will of others to work for peace and justice I will be satisfied.

I believe sincerely, because of the love I have known that a God of love is present no matter what the circumstances. I need no assurance of a "heaven" after death but do believe that our spirits live on in others and in the world.

I give thanks that I have had a satisfying and fruitful life and that I have been blessed by the love and support of my two brothers, Maurice and Ralph. My children, Dennis, Peter and Susan, have each found satisfying vocations with important social justice dimensions. My nine grandchildren, each in their own way, show indications of concerns for humanity and the world in which they live. Most of all I give thanks for the encompassing love of Doreen and Sheila and the support and encouragement they offered so unstintingly. What more can I ask?

Floyd with granddaughters, Hanah and Naomi

AFTERWORD

After a long battle with Non-Hodgekins Lymphoma, my father, Floyd Howlett, died on June 28, 2003, at home, surrounded by loving family and friends.

It was a real gift to be able to work with my father on this book project. Over a three year period he would draft chapters and we would discuss what he had written. Through the process I not only gained a deeper understanding of my father's life and faith journey, but I also discovered where many of my own political and faith convictions came from. My father was gentle and compassionate but also very determined. He continued to be active in working for justice right up to until the end. He went out to peace marches, even though he could only walk for a block or two. On the Sunday before he died he insisted on leading a bible study discussion at an Affirm meeting on the theme of Reconciliation. And he was determined to complete this book. The week before he died I was able to spend a long weekend with him going over the edited manuscript which we had received from the publisher. Although he would have liked to have been around for the book launching he could see from the draft layout that the book was becoming a reality.

I hope that this book will inspire readers to continue the work for peace and justice and inter-cultural and inter-faith understanding that was so important in my father's life. And I pray that it might make a contribution to the struggle for renewal of the church so that it might focus on witnessing to the call for love, peace and justice in the world rather than self-preservation.

Dennis Howlett

INDEX

A
Affleck, Rev. George 14-15, 16
Agnew, Dr. Gordon 9
Agnew, William 121

B
Beveridge family 17
Bott, Edith 20, 23, 24-25
Bott, Ernest 20, 24-25
Bowman, Clem 5
Brownlee, Helen and Wally 23, 26, 91
Buddhism 14, 79, 94, 147, 184, 186-188, 189, 190, 192, 193, 195, 196, 199

C
Calvin, John 159, 160
Canadian Girls in Training 19
Canadian Urban Training Program 3, 158
Carlton St. United Church 11, 12, 13
Clugston, Don and Ruth 27, 28, 37, 52
Cone, James 168-172, 206
Coon Come, Matthew 206

D
Dohoku Centre 37, 42, 51, 66, 71-75, 77, 92, 93-95, 96, 98, 101, 105, 109, 111, 113-115, 119, 134, 152, 153, 155, 156, 180, 194, 209; English school 86-88

E
Esterhazy Pastoral Charge 16-18, 20, 125, 126-127, 158

F
Fairbairn, Rev. Edis 6, 7-8, 11, 14, 16, 172, 203, 205, 207, 210, 211, 214
Finlay, Rev. James 8, 11-13, 203, 205
Flook, Vernon 17, 126
Frye, Prof. Northrop 13-14, 207-208

G
Graham family 19, 25-26, 39
Gutierrez, Gustavo 163-165

H
Hiura, Dr. Makoto 74, 77, 81-83, 85
Hoekendijk, J.C. 1, 209
Homma, Kimiko and Yoshimaro 84
Hosoumi, Rev. Mitsuko 66-69, 82, 94, 96-97, 135-136, 207
Howlett, Dennis 6, 23, 26, 28, 31, 32, 45, 53, 57, 105, 117, 127, 137, 138, 140, 142, 145, 150, 152-155, 173, 185, 199, 201, 218, 220
Howlett, Doreen 1, 2, 3, 6, 19, 22-23, 27, 31, 32, 34, 44, 45, 46, 52-54, 62, 65, 66, 86, 92, 101-105, 107, 118, 119, 120,

121-144, 145, 173, 183, 185, 199, 219
Howlett, Hilda 5-7, 16, 45-46, 51-54, 145
Howlett, Maurice 7, 32, 217, 218
Howlett, Peter 6, 26, 53, 105, 117-118, 137, 138, 142, 149-152, 201, 218
Howlett, Ralph 6, 7, 54, 141, 218
Howlett, Susan 26, 87, 105, 117-118, 132, 137, 140, 142, 143, 145-149, 150, 199, 201, 219
Howlett, Wesley 5-7, 16, 32, 51

I
Igarashi family 83-84

K
Kagawa, Rev. Toyohiko 37, 38, 42, 63, 73, 75-77, 112, 154, 156-157, 172, 203-205, 206, 209, 214
KAIROS: Canadian Ecumenical Justice Initiative ix, 152, 155, 201
Kawartha Ploughshares 141, 144, 199, 200, 205
Kim, Chi Ha 167-169, 180
Kimata, Rev. Toshi 38, 209
King, Martin Luther, Jr. 154, 161-163, 206
Koinonia Youth Group 90
Kubo, Michiko 84-86
Kumagai, Dr. Toyoji 113-114, 135, 136
Kurisu, Mr. 32, 53, 58, 91, 150, 151, 184-186
Kyodan 3, 18, 19, 29-30, 50, 51, 67, 72, 95, 101, 109, 118, 128, 158; Hokkaido District 41-42, 70

L
Lindsay, Ontario (*see also Nayoro-Lindsay Twinning*) 121, 122, 126, 141
Lowe, Jane 87
Luther, Martin 159-160

M
MacLeod, Virginia and Ian 27, 28, 31, 32
McLean, Alan 88, 142, 180
McLure, Dr. Bob 11
Minjun Theology 165-169, 180
Miyajima, Toshimitsu 84-86, 206
Mizushima, Chieko 89
Morwood, Gordon 86-88, 105, 138

N
Nabigon-Howlett, Sheila 144, 183, 199-202, 217-219
Nakamura, Rev. Mitsuo 42, 65, 73-75, 82, 90, 93, 94, 99, 101
Narita Airport 115-118, 134
Nayoro-Lindsay Twinning 101-105, 134, 187
Nettle, Mary Ellen 96-98
Nihon Kirisuto Kyodan (*see Kyodan*)
Niihori, Kunji 24, 48, 49
Nishizaki, Noriyoshi 100-101
Nopporo Agricultural College 43, 73, 74, 77, 81, 82, 83, 85, 113
Northern Hokkaido Christian Centre (*see Dohoku Centre*)

O
Oaten, Rev. Bev 9
O'Murchu, Dairmuid 213-214
Orth, Rev. Don 38, 46, 48

Index

Orton, Dr. Arnot 9
Overseas Mission Board 10, 18, 30, 34

P

Peterborough Coalition for Social Justice 215-217
Pioneer Evangelism Plan 41-42, 43, 44, 61, 67
Prairie Christian Training Centre 6, 92, 138-139, 169, 174, 181-182, 194, 195, 197, 199, 212

R

Rissho Koseikai 188, 190, 191-194
Romero, Archbishop Oscar 164
Ruether, Rosemary 174-176
Russell, Letty M. 174, 176-179

S

Saito, Koichi and Tamiko 99-100
Scott, Bert 15
Seicho No Ie 189-190
Shintoism 79, 184-186, 188, 189
Simons, Menno 160
Soka Gakkai 188, 190-191, 193
Stone, Alfred 20, 23, 24, 28, 30, 31, 33, 37, 38, 45-51, 70, 207
Stone, Jean 20, 23, 33, 45, 48-49
Student Christian Movement 13, 153, 207

T

Tamura, Rev. Kiyoji 27, 28, 33, 36, 37, 39, 41, 43, 52, 59, 61, 64, 67, 70, 71, 93, 173
Thompson, David 88-89
Tokyo Union Church 23, 26
Toyamaru 45-47

U

Uchimura, Kunzo 211
Uedo, Yoko 89
United Church of Canada 2, 3, 8, 9, 16, 20, 48, 71, 89, 173, 182, 183, 195, 210, 212; Bay of Quinte Conference 122, 142; Division of World Outreach 105, 122, 210; London Conference 107; Peterborough Presbetry 209
United Church of Christ in Japan (*see Kyodan*)
United Church Training School 121, 123

V

Von Kameke family 10-11

W

Walz, H.H. 161
Weatherhead, Dr. Leslie 15
West Montrose United Church 5, 7, 8, 15, 16
Witmer, Keiko 105-107, 114, 138
Witmer, Rob 48, 86, 105-107, 114, 138, 187
World Council of Churches ix, 159, 161

Y

Young People's Forward Movement 12, 15, 121
Young People's Union 6, 8-9, 13, 122

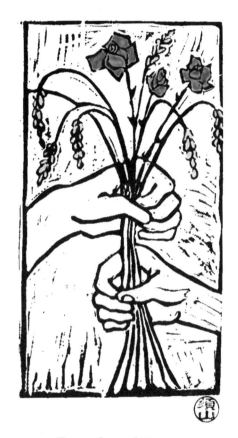

Bread and Roses
by Susan Howlett